Jewelry Making Book!

Suzanne J. Katts

Copyright © 2024 by Suzanne J. Katts

All rights reserved. No part of this publication may be reproduced, distributed, or transmitted in any form or by any means, including photocopying, recording, or other electronic or mechanical methods, without the prior written permission of the publisher, except in the case of brief quotations embodied in critical reviews and certain other noncommercial uses permitted by copyright law.

This book is intended for informational purposes only. The author and publisher have made every effort to ensure the accuracy of the information herein, but make no warranties or representations as to the accuracy, completeness, or suitability of the content. The information provided in this book is provided "as is" without warranty of any kind. The author and publisher shall not be liable for any loss, damage, or injury arising from the use of this book or the techniques described herein.

The techniques and projects described in this book involve working with potentially hazardous materials and tools. Readers are advised to exercise caution and follow all safety precautions recommended by manufacturers and experienced practitioners. The author and publisher disclaim any liability for injuries or accidents that may occur as a result of following the instructions provided in this book.

Any trademarks, service marks, product names, or company names mentioned in this book are used for identification purposes only and may be the property of their respective owners. The inclusion of such references does not imply endorsement or affiliation with the author or publisher.

While efforts have been made to respect the intellectual property rights of others, if any material included in this book infringes upon the rights of any third party, please contact the publisher so that appropriate corrections can be made in future editions.

For permission requests or inquiries about this book, please contact the publisher.

"Jewelry Making Book"

Chapter: Brief Overview of the Art of Jewelry Making 10

Chapter: Author's Background and Expertise in Jewelry Making 12

Chapter: Explanation of the Book's Structure and What Readers Can Expect 14

Chapter: Getting Started - Tools and Materials Needed for Jewelry Making 17

Chapter: Exploring Jewelry Making Techniques 20

Chapter: Setting Up Your Jewelry Making Workspace 23

Chapter: Beading Basics - Introduction to Different Types of Beads and Their Uses 26

Chapter: Step-by-Step Instructions for Basic Beading Techniques 29

Chapter: Stringing Beads 32

Chapter: Knotting Beads 35

Chapter: Bead Weaving 38

Chapter: Basic Wire Wrapping 41

Chapter: Beading Basics - Exploring Different Types of Beads 44

Chapter: Beading Basics - Step-by-Step Instructions 47

Chapter: Selecting the Right Beads for Your Projects 50

Chapter: Wirework Wonders: Introduction to Wireworking Tools and Materials 53

Chapter: Basic Wireworking Techniques: Step-by-Step Instructions 56

Chapter: Wire Wrapping 59

Chapter: Coiling 62

Chapter: Shaping 64

Chapter: Hammering 66

Chapter: Projects Incorporating Wirework 69

Chapter: Metal Magic: Overview of Metals in Jewelry Making 71

Chapter: Silver 74

Chapter: Gold: A Timeless Treasure in Jewelry Making 76

Chapter: Copper: Embracing Warmth and Character in Jewelry Making 78

Chapter: Brass: A Versatile Alloy in Jewelry Making 81

Chapter: Platinum: The Epitome of Elegance and Endurance 84

Chapter: Introduction to Metalworking Tools and Safety Precautions 87

Chapter: Basic Metalworking Techniques: A Step-by-Step Guide 90

Chapter: Soldering: Joining Metals with Precision and Strength 93

Chapter: Texturing: Adding Depth and Dimension to Metal Surfaces 95

Chapter: Forming: Shaping Metal into Three-Dimensional Masterpieces 97

Chapter: Piercing and Sawing: Precision Cutting for Intricate Designs 100

Chapter: Metalworking Projects: Transforming Metal into Wearable Art 103

Chapter: Stamped Bracelets: Personalized Wearable Art 105

Chapter: Hammered Rings: Crafting Unique Metal Masterpieces 108

Chapter: Gemstone Glamour: Exploring the World of Precious Stones 110

Chapter: Diamonds: The Epitome of Elegance and Brilliance 113

Chapter: Rubies: The Gemstone of Passion and Prosperity 116

Chapter: Sapphires: The Essence of Elegance and Versatility 119

Chapter: Emeralds: The Gemstone of Renewal and Splendor 122

Chapter: Other Gemstones: Exploring a World of Color and Splendor 125

Chapter: Pearls - Nature's Timeless Elegance 128

Chapter: Citrines - Sunshine in Gemstone Form 131

Chapter: Aquamarines - Gems of Tranquility and Clarity 134

Chapter: Gemstone Projects: Unleashing Radiance in Jewelry Designs 137

Chapter: Advanced Techniques: Pushing the Boundaries of Jewelry Making 140

Chapter: Enameling: Adding Vibrant Colors to Metal 143

Chapter: Etching: Unveiling the Beauty of Intricate Designs 145

Chapter: Granulation: Crafting Timeless Beauty with Tiny Granules 148

Chapter: Mokume Gane: Unveiling the Beauty of Layered Metals 151

Chapter: Mastering Advanced Jewelry Making Techniques 154

Chapter: Projects Showcasing the Versatility of Advanced Techniques 159

Chapter: Design and Inspiration 164

Chapter: Guidance on Developing a Personal Style 167

Chapter: Exercises and Prompts to Spark Creativity 170

Chapter: Finishing Touches 173

Chapter: Polishing 176

Chapter: Patina 179

Chapter: Oxidation 182

Chapter: Finishing Seals 185

Chapter: Tips for Properly Finishing and Presenting Jewelry Pieces 188

Chapter: Guidance on Pricing and Selling Handmade Jewelry 191

Conclusion: Recap of Key Concepts Covered in the Book 194

Chapter: Embrace Your Journey 196

Chapter: Suzanne J. Katts Speaks 198

Glossary of Jewelry Making Terms 200

JEWELRY MAMES 202

TEMPLATES 203

FUTURE BOOK TITLES 205

Chapter: Brief Overview of the Art of Jewelry Making

Jewelry making is an ancient and timeless art form that has captivated humanity for millennia. From adorning pharaohs in ancient Egypt to gracing the runways of haute couture, jewelry has always held a special place in our hearts, symbolizing status, beauty, and personal expression.

In this chapter, we embark on a journey into the enchanting world of jewelry making—a world where creativity knows no bounds and craftsmanship reigns supreme. Here, we'll explore the rich history and cultural significance of jewelry, from its earliest origins to its modern-day evolution.

Throughout history, jewelry has served a multitude of purposes beyond mere adornment. It has been worn as talismans for protection, as symbols of love and commitment, and as markers of social status and wealth. Each piece tells a story, reflecting the beliefs, values, and aesthetic sensibilities of its creator and wearer.

Today, jewelry making encompasses a wide range of techniques and materials, from traditional metalsmithing and gemstone cutting to contemporary approaches like wirework and bead weaving. Whether you're drawn to the luster of precious metals, the brilliance of gemstones, or the tactile allure of beads, there's a jewelry-making technique to suit every taste and style.

In the following chapters, we'll delve into the fundamentals of jewelry making, exploring the tools, materials, and techniques that form the foundation of this art form. From basic bead stringing to advanced metalworking, each chapter will provide step-by-step instructions and creative inspiration to help you unleash your inner artisan and craft exquisite jewelry pieces that reflect your unique vision and personality.

So, join me as we embark on this journey of discovery and creativity. Whether you're a novice or a seasoned jeweler, there's always something new to learn and explore in the ever-evolving world of jewelry making. Let your imagination soar, and let's create brilliance together.

Chapter: Author's Background and Expertise in Jewelry Making

Welcome to this chapter, where we'll delve into the background and expertise of the author, Suzanne J. Katts, in the captivating world of jewelry making. Suzanne's journey as a jewelry artisan is not only a testament to her passion for the craft but also a source of inspiration for aspiring jewelers worldwide.

Suzanne's fascination with jewelry began at a young age, sparked by her grandmother's vintage jewelry collection and her mother's love for crafting. As a child, she would spend hours admiring the intricate details of each piece, marveling at the way they shimmered and sparkled in the light.

Driven by her passion for creativity and craftsmanship, Suzanne pursued formal training in jewelry making, studying under master jewelers and artisans to hone her skills. Through years of dedication and practice, she mastered a wide range of techniques, from traditional metalsmithing to contemporary bead weaving, and developed her unique artistic style.

Drawing inspiration from nature, art, and culture, Suzanne infuses her jewelry designs with a sense of elegance, whimsy, and timeless beauty. Her pieces are characterized by meticulous attention to detail, exquisite craftsmanship, and a deep appreciation for the inherent beauty of materials.

Beyond her work as a jeweler, Suzanne is also an educator and mentor, passionate about sharing her knowledge and inspiring others to explore their creativity through jewelry making. Through workshops, classes, and online tutorials, she empowers aspiring jewelers to unleash their creativity and express themselves through the art of jewelry making.

In this chapter, Suzanne will share insights into her journey as a jewelry artisan, including her creative process, sources of inspiration, and the lessons she's learned along the way. Whether you're a beginner looking to explore the world of jewelry making or an experienced jeweler seeking to expand your skills, Suzanne's expertise and guidance will inspire you to embark on your own creative journey and craft jewelry pieces that resonate with beauty, meaning, and craftsmanship. So, let's dive in and discover the story behind the artisan— Suzanne J. Katts.

Chapter: Explanation of the Book's Structure and What Readers Can Expect

Welcome to this chapter, where we'll provide you with a roadmap to navigate through "Jewelry Making Book: A Comprehensive Guide to Jewelry Making." In this section, we'll outline the structure of the book and give you a glimpse of what you can expect as you embark on your journey into the captivating world of jewelry making.

"Jewelry Making Book" is divided into several chapters, each focusing on different aspects of jewelry making, from basic techniques to advanced skills, design principles, and business essentials. Here's a brief overview of what you'll find in each chapter:

Chapter: Getting Started
In this chapter, we'll cover the essentials of jewelry making, including the tools and materials you'll need to get started, as well as an introduction to different types of jewelry making techniques. Whether you're new to the craft or a seasoned jeweler, this chapter will help you set up your workspace and lay the foundation for your creative journey.

Chapter: Beading Basics
Explore the world of beads and learn basic beading techniques such as stringing and knotting. This chapter is perfect for beginners who want to dive into the art of beadwork and create stunning beaded jewelry pieces.

Chapter: Wirework Wonders

Discover the versatility of wire as we delve into basic wireworking techniques such as wire wrapping and coiling. From elegant wire-wrapped pendants to intricate wirework designs, this chapter will inspire you to explore the endless possibilities of wire in your jewelry making projects.

Chapter: Metal Magic

Enter the realm of metalsmithing and learn how to work with metals to create beautiful jewelry pieces. From soldering and texturing to forming and finishing, this chapter will guide you through the fundamentals of metalworking and help you bring your metal jewelry designs to life.

Chapter: Gemstone Glamour

Uncover the allure of gemstones and learn how to incorporate them into your jewelry designs. From selecting and caring for gemstones to setting them in metal, this chapter will teach you everything you need to know to create breathtaking gemstone jewelry pieces.

Chapter: Advanced Techniques

Take your jewelry making skills to the next level with advanced techniques such as enameling, etching, and stone setting. This chapter is perfect for experienced jewelers looking to expand their repertoire and explore new avenues of creativity.

Chapter: Design and Inspiration

Discover the secrets of design excellence and find inspiration for your jewelry designs. From developing your unique artistic voice to cultivating your design skills, this chapter will help you unlock your creative potential and create jewelry pieces that truly reflect your personality and style.

Chapter: Finishing Touches

Learn how to put the final polish on your jewelry pieces with techniques such as polishing, patina, and presentation. This chapter will guide you through the finishing touches that will elevate your jewelry pieces from ordinary to extraordinary.

And many more!

Conclusion
In the final chapter of the book, we'll recap key concepts covered throughout the book and offer words of encouragement and inspiration as you continue on your jewelry making journey. Whether you're a hobbyist or aspiring professional, this chapter will leave you feeling inspired and ready to unleash your creativity.

Throughout the book, you'll find step-by-step instructions, helpful tips, and vibrant illustrations to guide you through each technique and project. Whether you're a beginner or an experienced jeweler, "Jewelry Making Book" is your comprehensive guide to creating beautiful, one-of-a-kind jewelry pieces that reflect your unique style and personality.

So, are you ready to embark on your journey into the enchanting world of jewelry making? Let's dive in and start Jewelry Making together.

Chapter: Getting Started - Tools and Materials Needed for Jewelry Making

Welcome to the exciting world of jewelry making! In this chapter, we'll take you through the essential tools and materials you'll need to begin your journey as a jewelry artisan. Whether you're a complete novice or a seasoned crafter, having the right tools and materials at your disposal is crucial for creating beautiful and enduring jewelry pieces.

Tools:

Pliers: Pliers are indispensable tools for jewelry making, used for bending, shaping, and manipulating wire and metal components. Essential types of pliers include:

Round-nose pliers: Ideal for creating loops and curves in wire.
Chain-nose pliers: Used for gripping and bending wire, as well as opening and closing jump rings.
Flat-nose pliers: Perfect for gripping and bending flat pieces of metal or wire.
Wire Cutters: Wire cutters are essential for cutting wire, headpins, and other metal components to the desired length. Look for a pair with sharp, precise blades for clean cuts.

Flush Cutters: Flush cutters are specialized wire cutters that leave a flat, even cut on wire, eliminating sharp edges that can snag on clothing or skin.

Beading Needles: Beading needles are thin, flexible needles used for stringing beads onto thread or wire. They come in various sizes to accommodate different types of beads and stringing materials.

Jewelry Hammer: A jewelry hammer is used for texturing metal, shaping wire, and riveting components together. Choose a hammer with a comfortable grip and different head sizes for versatility.

Materials:

Beads: Beads come in a wide variety of shapes, sizes, colors, and materials, including glass, gemstone, metal, and polymer clay. Choose beads that complement your design aesthetic and fit the theme of your project.

Wire: Wire is a versatile material used in various jewelry making techniques, including wire wrapping, wire weaving, and wire soldering. Different types of wire include:

Sterling silver wire
Gold-filled wire
Copper wire
Craft wire (e.g., artistic wire)
Findings: Findings are essential components used to finish and secure jewelry pieces. Common types of findings include:

Jump rings
Lobster clasps
Ear wires
Crimp beads and clasps
Metals: Metals such as sterling silver, gold, copper, and brass are commonly used in jewelry making. These metals can be formed, soldered, textured, and polished to create stunning jewelry pieces.

Stringing Materials: Stringing materials such as beading wire, silk thread, and leather cord are used to string beads and create jewelry designs. Choose a stringing material that complements your beads and provides durability for your finished piece.

As you begin your jewelry making journey, start with a basic toolkit and gradually expand your collection of tools and materials as you explore new techniques and projects. With the right tools and materials at your disposal, the possibilities for creating beautiful, one-of-a-kind jewelry pieces are endless. So, gather your supplies, and let's start Jewelry Making together!

Chapter: Exploring Jewelry Making Techniques

In this chapter, we'll explore the diverse array of techniques used in jewelry making, from the delicate art of beading to the intricate craftsmanship of metalwork. Each technique offers its own unique challenges and opportunities for creativity, allowing jewelry artisans to express themselves in a myriad of ways. Let's dive into the world of jewelry making techniques and discover the possibilities they hold.

Beading:
Beading is one of the most accessible and versatile jewelry making techniques, suitable for crafters of all skill levels. It involves stringing beads onto a thread or wire to create necklaces, bracelets, earrings, and more. Beads come in a wide variety of materials, shapes, sizes, and colors, allowing for endless combinations and designs. Basic beading techniques include stringing, knotting, and weaving, while more advanced techniques include bead embroidery and bead stitching.

Wirework:
Wirework is a technique that involves manipulating wire to create intricate designs and structures in jewelry. Common wirework techniques include wire wrapping, wire weaving, and wire sculpting. Wire can be shaped, twisted, and coiled to form intricate patterns, frames, and embellishments. Wirework is often used to create pendants, earrings, rings, and intricate components for beaded jewelry.

Metalwork:

Metalwork is the art of shaping, forming, and manipulating metal to create jewelry pieces. Techniques in metalwork include soldering, forging, texturing, and casting. Metals such as sterling silver, gold, copper, and brass are commonly used in metalwork, each offering its own unique properties and aesthetic qualities. Metalwork allows artisans to create durable and enduring jewelry pieces with intricate details and textures.

Enameling:
Enameling is a decorative technique that involves fusing powdered glass to metal surfaces through high heat. The result is a vibrant and durable surface that adds color and depth to jewelry pieces. Enameling techniques include cloisonné, champlevé, and plique-à-jour, each requiring precision and skill to achieve stunning results. Enameling can be used to embellish metal jewelry components or create standalone enamel pieces.

Stone Setting:
Stone setting is the process of securing gemstones into metal settings to create jewelry pieces. Common stone setting techniques include prong setting, bezel setting, and channel setting. Stone setting requires precision and attention to detail to ensure that gemstones are securely held in place while allowing them to sparkle and shine. Stone setting can be combined with other techniques such as metalwork and wirework to create elaborate and intricate designs.

Mixed Media:

Mixed media jewelry making involves combining different materials and techniques to create unique and eclectic jewelry pieces. Materials such as textiles, found objects, resin, and polymer clay can be incorporated into jewelry designs to add texture, color, and dimension. Mixed media jewelry making allows artisans to experiment with unconventional materials and techniques, resulting in truly one-of-a-kind wearable art pieces.

Each jewelry making technique offers its own set of challenges and rewards, inviting artisans to explore their creativity and push the boundaries of their craft. Whether you're drawn to the delicate intricacy of beadwork, the bold elegance of metalwork, or the whimsical charm of mixed media, there's a jewelry making technique to suit every style and aesthetic. So, experiment, explore, and let your imagination soar as you embark on your jewelry making journey!

Chapter: Setting Up Your Jewelry Making Workspace

Creating a dedicated and organized workspace is essential for anyone venturing into the world of jewelry making. A well-equipped and comfortable workspace not only enhances creativity but also ensures safety and efficiency. In this chapter, we'll provide you with valuable tips for setting up your jewelry making workspace, whether it's a designated studio or a corner of your home.

Choose the Right Location:

Select a quiet and well-lit area in your home where you can set up your jewelry making workspace. Natural light is ideal, but if that's not possible, invest in good quality task lighting to illuminate your work area.
Ensure that your workspace is away from high-traffic areas and distractions to help you stay focused and productive.
Invest in Essential Tools and Equipment:

Acquire the necessary tools and equipment for your jewelry making projects, including pliers, wire cutters, bead mats, and a workbench or sturdy table.
Organize your tools and supplies in a way that makes them easily accessible and visible. Consider using pegboards, drawer organizers, or storage bins to keep your workspace clutter-free.
Prioritize Safety:

Familiarize yourself with safety practices and precautions for working with tools and materials commonly used in jewelry making.
Wear appropriate safety gear, such as safety glasses and gloves, when handling sharp tools or working with chemicals.
Keep a first aid kit nearby in case of accidents or injuries.
Create an Inspiring Environment:

Personalize your workspace with inspiring decor, artwork, or photographs that reflect your style and aesthetic.
Display samples of your past work or favorite jewelry pieces to serve as a source of inspiration and motivation.
Organize Your Supplies:

Keep your beads, findings, and other materials neatly organized and labeled for easy access. Consider using storage containers, jars, or compartmentalized trays to sort and store your supplies.
Invest in a bead organizer or bead storage system to keep your bead collection organized and prevent them from rolling away.
Designate Work Areas:

Create separate work areas for different stages of the jewelry making process, such as a soldering station, a bead stringing area, and a wirework station.
Keep each work area clean and clutter-free to minimize distractions and maximize productivity.
Practice Good Ergonomics:

Set up your workspace in a way that promotes good posture and reduces strain on your body. Ensure that your workbench or table is at a comfortable height and that your tools and materials are within easy reach.
Invest in an ergonomic chair or stool that provides support and comfort during long periods of jewelry making.

By following these tips, you can create a functional and inspiring workspace that will enhance your creativity and productivity as you embark on your jewelry making journey. Whether you're a beginner or an experienced jeweler, having a well-equipped and organized workspace is key to unlocking your full potential as a jewelry artisan. So, roll up your sleeves, gather your tools, and let's get creative!

Chapter: Beading Basics - Introduction to Different Types of Beads and Their Uses

Welcome to the colorful and creative world of beading! In this chapter, we'll introduce you to the wide variety of beads available to jewelry makers and explore their unique characteristics and uses. Whether you're a beginner or an experienced beader, understanding the different types of beads will expand your design possibilities and inspire your creativity.

Seed Beads:

Seed beads are tiny, uniformly shaped beads that come in a range of sizes, from the smallest 15/0 to larger 6/0 beads. These beads are commonly used for bead weaving, bead embroidery, and intricate beadwork stitches such as peyote stitch and brick stitch.
Seed beads are available in various materials, including glass, metal, and plastic, and come in a wide array of colors and finishes.
Czech Glass Beads:

Czech glass beads are renowned for their high quality and craftsmanship, and they come in a variety of shapes, sizes, and colors.
These beads are popular for their versatility and are used in a wide range of jewelry making techniques, including stringing, bead weaving, and bead embroidery.
Gemstone Beads:

Gemstone beads are natural or synthetic stones that have been shaped and polished into beads for use in jewelry making. Each gemstone has its own unique properties and characteristics, making them highly sought after for their beauty and metaphysical properties.
Gemstone beads can be used as focal points in jewelry designs or combined with other beads to add color and texture.
Crystal Beads:

Crystal beads, made from leaded glass, are prized for their brilliance and sparkle. They come in a variety of shapes, sizes, and colors, including clear, AB (aurora borealis), and coated finishes.
These beads are commonly used as accents in jewelry designs, adding a touch of elegance and glamour to any piece.
Metal Beads:

Metal beads come in a variety of finishes, including sterling silver, gold-filled, brass, and copper.
These beads can be plain or decorative, with designs ranging from simple spacer beads to ornate filigree and granulated beads.
Metal beads are often used as accents in jewelry designs, adding texture, shine, and visual interest.
Polymer Clay Beads:

Polymer clay beads are handmade beads crafted from polymer clay, a versatile and colorful medium.
These beads can be molded, shaped, and embellished in endless ways, making them perfect for creating unique and personalized jewelry pieces.
Pearls:

Pearls are organic gemstones formed inside the shells of certain mollusks, such as oysters and mussels.

These lustrous beads come in a variety of shapes, sizes, and colors, ranging from classic white to exotic shades of black and peacock.

Pearls are prized for their timeless elegance and are commonly used in bridal jewelry and other special occasion pieces.

By familiarizing yourself with the different types of beads available, you'll be able to choose the perfect beads for your jewelry designs and create stunning pieces that reflect your personal style and creativity. So, let your imagination soar as you explore the endless possibilities of beadwork and unleash your inner bead artist!

Chapter: Step-by-Step Instructions for Basic Beading Techniques

In this chapter, we'll guide you through the fundamental beading techniques that form the building blocks of many jewelry designs. Whether you're a beginner or looking to refresh your skills, mastering these basic techniques will give you the confidence and knowledge to create beautiful beaded jewelry pieces. Let's dive in!

Stringing Beads:
Stringing beads is one of the simplest and most versatile beading techniques, perfect for creating necklaces, bracelets, and anklets. Follow these steps to string beads onto beading wire or thread:

Cut a length of beading wire or thread slightly longer than your desired finished length, allowing extra for knots and closures.
Attach a clasp to one end of the wire or thread using crimp beads or a jump ring.
String your desired beads onto the wire or thread in the desired pattern or arrangement.
Once all beads are strung, attach the other end of the clasp using crimp beads or a jump ring, and secure it in place with crimping pliers.
Trim any excess wire or thread, and your beaded strand is ready to wear!
Knotting Beads:

Knotting beads is a traditional technique used to create knotted strands of beads, commonly seen in pearl necklaces and mala beads. Here's how to knot beads using silk cord:

Cut a length of silk cord slightly longer than your desired finished length, allowing extra for knots and closures.
Thread a bead onto the silk cord, leaving a small tail at the end.
Tie an overhand knot tightly against the bead, securing it in place.
Repeat the process, adding beads and knotting between each bead until your strand is complete.
Attach a clasp to each end of the strand using knot covers or clamshell bead tips, and secure with crimping pliers.
Trim any excess cord, and your knotted bead strand is ready to wear!
Bead Weaving:
Bead weaving is a technique that involves stitching together beads to create intricate patterns and designs. One of the most basic bead weaving stitches is the peyote stitch:

Start by threading a needle with beading thread and attaching a stop bead a few inches from the end.
Pick up an even number of beads, and stitch back through the first bead to form a loop.
Pick up another bead, and stitch through the next bead in the previous row.
Continue adding beads and stitching through the previous row until your desired length is reached.
To add rows, start each new row by stitching through the first bead of the previous row, and continue stitching in the same manner.
Finish your beadwork by weaving in the thread ends and attaching a clasp or finishing component.
Basic Wire Wrapping:

Wire wrapping is a versatile technique used to create loops and connections with wire. Here's how to make a simple wire-wrapped loop:

Cut a length of wire and use round-nose pliers to create a small loop at one end.
Thread a bead onto the wire, and use chain-nose pliers to bend the wire at a right angle just above the bead.
Use round-nose pliers to grip the wire just above the bend, and wrap the wire around the pliers to create a second loop.
Continue wrapping the wire around itself to form a coil, stopping when you reach the bead.
Trim any excess wire, and use chain-nose pliers to tuck in the end of the wire to secure it in place.
Your wire-wrapped bead is now ready to be incorporated into your jewelry design!

By mastering these basic beading techniques, you'll have the skills and confidence to create a wide variety of beaded jewelry pieces. Whether you're stringing beads onto wire, knotting strands of pearls, weaving intricate patterns, or wire-wrapping beads, the possibilities for creativity are endless. So, gather your beads and tools, and let your imagination soar as you explore the art of beadwork!

Chapter: Stringing Beads

Stringing beads is a fundamental technique in jewelry making, offering endless possibilities for creating beautiful and versatile pieces. Whether you're designing a simple necklace, a statement bracelet, or an elegant anklet, mastering the art of stringing beads will open up a world of creativity. In this chapter, we'll walk you through the step-by-step process of stringing beads onto beading wire or thread, ensuring that your finished piece is both secure and stylish.

Gather Your Materials:
Before you begin, gather your materials:

Beads of your choice
Beading wire or thread
Clasp (such as a lobster clasp or spring ring clasp)
Jump rings
Crimp beads
Crimping pliers
Wire cutters
Bead design board or flat surface
Measure and Cut Your Beading Wire or Thread:
Determine the desired length of your finished piece and cut a length of beading wire or thread slightly longer than this measurement. It's always better to have a little extra length to work with than to come up short.

Attach the Clasp:

Thread one end of the beading wire or thread through the loop of your clasp.

Slide a crimp bead onto the wire or thread, followed by a jump ring.
Pass the end of the wire or thread back through the crimp bead, creating a loop around the jump ring and clasp.
Use crimping pliers to gently squeeze the crimp bead, securing it in place. Be careful not to crush the crimp bead completely, as this may weaken the connection.

String Your Beads:

Plan out the design or pattern for your piece before you begin stringing beads. You can lay out your beads on a bead design board or simply visualize the arrangement in your mind.
Start stringing beads onto the wire or thread, following your chosen pattern or arrangement. You can use your fingers to slide the beads into place, or use a beading needle for smaller beads or tighter spaces.

Finish with the Clasp:

Once you have strung all of your beads onto the wire or thread, it's time to finish the piece.
Thread the end of the wire or thread through the loop of the other half of your clasp.
Slide a crimp bead onto the wire or thread, followed by a jump ring.
Pass the end of the wire or thread back through the crimp bead, creating a loop around the jump ring and clasp.
Use crimping pliers to gently squeeze the crimp bead, securing it in place.
Trim any excess wire or thread using wire cutters.

Final Touches:

Once your clasp is securely attached and the excess wire or thread is trimmed, give your piece a final inspection to ensure everything is secure and in place.
Gently tug on the beads to make sure they are properly strung and the clasp is secure.

Your beaded strand is now ready to wear or incorporate into your jewelry design!

Stringing beads is a versatile and accessible technique that allows you to create beautiful jewelry pieces with ease. Whether you're a beginner or an experienced jewelry maker, mastering the art of stringing beads will open up a world of creative possibilities. So, gather your materials and let your imagination soar as you design and string your own stunning bead creations!

Chapter: Knotting Beads

Knotting beads is a timeless and elegant technique that adds beauty and durability to your jewelry pieces. Whether you're creating a classic pearl necklace or a bohemian-inspired mala bead bracelet, knotting beads allows you to showcase each individual bead while ensuring they remain securely in place. In this chapter, we'll guide you through the step-by-step process of knotting beads using silk cord, resulting in a stunning knotted bead strand that's ready to wear.

Gather Your Materials:
Before you begin knotting beads, gather the following materials:

Beads of your choice
Silk cord (size appropriate for your beads)
Clasp (such as a lobster clasp or spring ring clasp)
Knot covers or clamshell bead tips
Crimping pliers
Scissors or wire cutters
Measure and Cut Your Silk Cord:

Determine the desired length of your finished piece and cut a length of silk cord slightly longer than this measurement. It's important to leave extra length for knots and closures, so don't cut the cord too short.
Thread the First Bead:

Thread one end of the silk cord through the hole of your first bead, leaving a small tail (approximately 1-2 inches) at the end. This tail will be used to tie knots later.
Tie the First Knot:

Hold the bead in place against the end of the cord and tie an overhand knot tightly against the bead. Ensure that the knot is snug against the bead to prevent it from slipping.
Add More Beads and Knots:

Thread additional beads onto the cord, leaving a small gap between each bead.
After each bead, tie a tight overhand knot against it to secure it in place. Be sure to maintain consistent spacing between knots for a uniform look.
Continue Knotting:

Repeat the process of adding beads and knotting between each bead until your strand is complete. Take your time and work carefully to ensure each knot is tight and secure.
Attach the Clasp:

Once you have finished knotting the beads, it's time to attach the clasp.
Thread both ends of the silk cord through a knot cover or clamshell bead tip.
Use crimping pliers to gently squeeze the cover or tip closed, securing the ends of the cord, and creating a neat finish.
Attach a clasp to each end of the strand using jump rings or split rings, and secure them closed with crimping pliers.
Trim Excess Cord:

Trim any excess cord close to the knot covers or clamshell bead tips using scissors or wire cutters. Be careful not to cut the knots or damage the beads.
Final Inspection:

Give your knotted bead strand a final inspection to ensure all knots are tight and secure, and the clasp is properly attached. Gently tug on the beads to make sure they are securely knotted in place.

Your knotted bead strand is now ready to wear and enjoy! Knotting beads is a rewarding technique that adds both beauty and strength to your jewelry designs. Whether you're creating a classic pearl necklace or a modern beaded bracelet, mastering the art of knotting beads will allow you to create stunning pieces that stand the test of time. So, gather your materials and let your creativity flow as you knot your own beautiful bead creations!

Chapter: Bead Weaving

Bead weaving is a captivating and intricate technique that allows you to create stunning jewelry pieces by stitching together beads in elaborate patterns and designs. From delicate bracelets to intricate tapestries, bead weaving offers endless possibilities for creativity and expression. In this chapter, we'll explore one of the most basic bead weaving stitches — the peyote stitch — and guide you through the step-by-step process of creating your own bead-woven masterpiece.

Gather Your Materials:
Before you begin bead weaving, gather the following materials:

Beads of your choice
Beading needle
Beading thread (such as Nymo or Fireline)
Scissors
Clasp or finishing component
Bead design board or flat surface
Thread the Needle and Attach a Stop Bead:

Thread your beading needle with a length of beading thread, leaving a tail several inches long.
Attach a stop bead to the tail of the thread by passing the needle through the bead twice, leaving a small loop at the end.
Start the First Row:

Pick up an even number of beads onto your needle, depending on the desired width of your beadwork. These beads will form the first row of your peyote stitch.

Stitch back through the first bead in the row, forming a loop with the beads.
Add Beads and Stitch the Second Row:

Pick up another bead onto your needle and stitch through the next bead in the previous row.
Continue adding beads and stitching through the beads in the previous row until you reach the end of the row.
Continue Adding Rows:

To add additional rows, start each new row by stitching through the first bead of the previous row.
Pick up beads and stitch through the beads in the previous row, following the pattern established in the first row.
Continue adding rows until your beadwork reaches the desired length.
Finish Your Beadwork:

Once you've completed your beadwork, weave the thread back through the beadwork to secure it in place.
Trim any excess thread, leaving a small tail.
Attach a clasp or finishing component to complete your beadwork and secure it for wearing.
Experiment with Variations:

Once you've mastered the basic peyote stitch, experiment with variations such as odd-count peyote or circular peyote to create different effects and designs.
Explore different bead sizes, shapes, and colors to customize your beadwork and add visual interest.

Bead weaving is a versatile and rewarding technique that offers endless opportunities for creativity and exploration. Whether you're a beginner or an experienced bead weaver, mastering the peyote stitch will open up a world of possibilities for creating beautiful jewelry pieces and intricate beadwork designs. So, gather your materials, thread your needle, and let your imagination soar as you weave your own stunning bead creations!

Chapter: Basic Wire Wrapping

Wire wrapping is a versatile and essential technique in jewelry making, allowing you to create secure connections, decorative elements, and unique designs with wire. Whether you're embellishing beads, creating pendants, or connecting components, mastering basic wire wrapping skills will elevate your jewelry designs to new heights. In this chapter, we'll focus on one of the most fundamental wire wrapping techniques—the simple wire-wrapped loop—and guide you through the process of creating your own wire-wrapped beads.

Gather Your Materials:
Before you begin wire wrapping, gather the following materials:

Wire of your choice (such as copper, sterling silver, or gold-filled wire)
Bead or component to wrap
Round-nose pliers
Chain-nose pliers
Wire cutters
Cut and Shape the Wire:

Cut a length of wire using wire cutters, ensuring it is long enough to create your desired wrapped loop and any additional decorative elements.
Use round-nose pliers to grip the end of the wire and create a small loop. Position the pliers near the end of the wire and rotate them to form a loop.
Thread the Bead:

Slide the bead or component onto the straight section of the wire, allowing it to rest against the loop you created.
Bend the Wire:

Use chain-nose pliers to grip the wire just above the bead, creating a right angle bend in the wire.
Ensure that the wire is bent securely against the bead to hold it in place.
Create the Second Loop:

Switch back to round-nose pliers and grip the wire just above the bend.
Rotate the pliers to create a second loop, mirroring the size and shape of the first loop.
Form the Coil:

Continue wrapping the wire around itself, forming a coil between the two loops. Wrap the wire tightly and evenly, working your way up towards the top loop.
Trim Excess Wire:

Once you have wrapped enough wire to form a secure coil, use wire cutters to trim any excess wire, leaving a small tail.
Secure the End:

Use chain-nose pliers to gently tuck in the end of the wire, securing it against the coil and preventing any sharp edges.
Final Inspection:

Give your wire-wrapped bead a final inspection, ensuring that all loops are securely closed, and the wire is neatly wrapped. Gently tug on the bead to test its stability and ensure that the wire is securely attached.
Your wire-wrapped bead is now ready to be incorporated into your jewelry design!

By mastering the basic wire wrapping technique of creating a simple wire-wrapped loop, you'll have the skills and confidence to add decorative elements, connectors, and embellishments to your jewelry designs. Experiment with different wire gauges, bead sizes, and wrapping styles to create unique and personalized pieces that showcase your creativity and craftsmanship. So, gather your materials and tools, and let your imagination soar as you explore the endless possibilities of wire wrapping in your jewelry making journey!

Chapter: Beading Basics - Exploring Different Types of Beads

Beads are the heart and soul of jewelry making, offering endless possibilities for creativity, expression, and personalization. From dazzling crystals to natural gemstones, each type of bead brings its own unique beauty and characteristics to your designs. In this chapter, we'll embark on a journey through the vast and colorful world of beads, exploring their diverse materials, shapes, sizes, and uses.

Seed Beads:
Seed beads are tiny, uniformly shaped beads that come in a wide range of sizes, from the smallest 15/0 to larger 6/0 beads. These beads are commonly used for intricate beadwork stitches such as peyote stitch, brick stitch, and loom weaving. They are available in various materials, including glass, metal, and plastic, and come in an array of colors, finishes, and coatings.

Czech Glass Beads:
Renowned for their high quality and craftsmanship, Czech glass beads come in a variety of shapes, sizes, and colors. From classic round beads to intricate pressed shapes and multi-faceted fire-polished beads, Czech glass beads are beloved by jewelry makers for their versatility and affordability. They are suitable for a wide range of techniques, including stringing, bead weaving, and bead embroidery.

Gemstone Beads:

Gemstone beads are natural or synthetic stones that have been shaped and polished into beads for use in jewelry making. Each gemstone has its own unique properties, colors, and patterns, making them highly sought after for their beauty and metaphysical qualities. From timeless classics like amethyst and turquoise to exotic stones like labradorite and larimar, gemstone beads add depth, color, and symbolism to jewelry designs.

Crystal Beads:
Crystal beads, made from leaded glass, are prized for their brilliance, sparkle, and clarity. Available in a wide range of shapes, sizes, and colors, crystal beads are perfect for adding glamour and elegance to any jewelry piece. Whether you're creating a statement necklace, a pair of dazzling earrings, or a sparkling bracelet, crystal beads are sure to catch the eye and capture the light.

Metal Beads:
Metal beads come in a variety of finishes, including sterling silver, gold-filled, brass, and copper. These beads can be plain or decorative, with designs ranging from simple spacer beads to ornate filigree and granulated beads. Metal beads are often used as accents in jewelry designs, adding texture, shine, and visual interest.

Polymer Clay Beads:
Polymer clay beads are handmade beads crafted from polymer clay, a versatile and colorful medium. These beads can be molded, shaped, and embellished in endless ways, making them perfect for creating unique and personalized jewelry pieces. From whimsical shapes and patterns to intricate textures and surface treatments, polymer clay beads offer endless possibilities for creativity and expression.

Pearls:

Pearls are organic gemstones formed inside the shells of certain mollusks, such as oysters and mussels. Prized for their luster, iridescence, and timeless elegance, pearls come in a variety of shapes, sizes, and colors, ranging from classic white to exotic shades of black and peacock. Whether you're creating a classic strand of pearls or incorporating them into a modern design, pearls add sophistication and refinement to any jewelry piece.

Each type of bead offers its own unique beauty, characteristics, and potential for creativity. By exploring the diverse world of beads and experimenting with different materials, shapes, and colors, you'll discover endless opportunities to create stunning and personalized jewelry pieces that reflect your style, passion, and imagination. So, gather your beads and let your creativity flow as you embark on your beading journey!

Chapter: Beading Basics - Step-by-Step Instructions

In this chapter, we'll cover the foundational techniques of beadwork, including stringing, knotting, and basic wire wrapping. These techniques serve as the building blocks for creating beautiful and intricate jewelry pieces. Whether you're a beginner or looking to refine your skills, mastering these basic beading techniques will empower you to bring your creative visions to life. Let's dive in!

Stringing Beads:
Stringing beads is one of the most versatile and accessible techniques in beadwork, suitable for creating a wide range of jewelry pieces, from simple bracelets to elaborate necklaces. Here's how to string beads onto beading wire or thread:

Cut a length of beading wire or thread slightly longer than your desired finished length, allowing extra for knots and closures.
Attach a clasp to one end of the wire or thread using crimp beads or a jump ring.
String your desired beads onto the wire or thread in the desired pattern or arrangement.
Once all beads are strung, attach the other end of the clasp using crimp beads or a jump ring, and secure it in place with crimping pliers.
Trim any excess wire or thread, and your beaded strand is ready to wear!
Knotting Beads:

Knotting beads is a traditional technique used to create knotted strands of beads, commonly seen in pearl necklaces and mala beads. Here's how to knot beads using silk cord:

Cut a length of silk cord slightly longer than your desired finished length, allowing extra for knots and closures.
Thread a bead onto the silk cord, leaving a small tail at the end.
Tie an overhand knot tightly against the bead, securing it in place.
Repeat the process, adding beads and knotting between each bead until your strand is complete.
Attach a clasp to each end of the strand using knot covers or clamshell bead tips, and secure with crimping pliers.
Trim any excess cord, and your knotted bead strand is ready to wear!

Basic Wire Wrapping:
Wire wrapping is a versatile technique used to create loops and connections with wire. Here's how to make a simple wire-wrapped loop:

Cut a length of wire and use round-nose pliers to create a small loop at one end.
Thread a bead onto the wire, and use chain-nose pliers to bend the wire at a right angle just above the bead.
Use round-nose pliers to grip the wire just above the bend, and wrap the wire around the pliers to create a second loop.
Continue wrapping the wire around itself to form a coil, stopping when you reach the bead.
Trim any excess wire, and use chain-nose pliers to tuck in the end of the wire to secure it in place.
Your wire-wrapped bead is now ready to be incorporated into your jewelry design!

By mastering these basic beading techniques, you'll have the skills and confidence to create a wide variety of jewelry pieces, from simple stringing projects to intricate beadwork designs. Experiment with different beads, wires, and techniques to unleash your creativity and express your unique style through beadwork. So, gather your materials and tools, and let's get started on your beading journey!

Chapter: Selecting the Right Beads for Your Projects

Choosing the perfect beads for your jewelry projects is an exciting and creative process. With countless shapes, sizes, colors, and materials to choose from, selecting the right beads can make a significant impact on the final look and feel of your design. In this chapter, we'll provide guidance on how to choose beads that complement your project and achieve the desired aesthetic.

Consider the Project Type:

Different jewelry projects require different types of beads. For example, if you're making a delicate necklace, you might opt for small, lightweight beads like seed beads or freshwater pearls. For a bold statement bracelet, larger beads with vibrant colors and intricate patterns may be more suitable.
Match Beads to Design Style:

Consider the overall style and theme of your design. Are you going for a bohemian, rustic look, or a modern, minimalist aesthetic? Choose beads that reflect and enhance the style you're aiming to achieve. For example, natural gemstone beads and wood beads are perfect for a bohemian vibe, while sleek glass or metal beads are ideal for a contemporary look.
Coordinate Colors and Finishes:

Select beads that complement each other in terms of color and finish. If your design features multiple bead colors, choose shades that harmonize well together or create an intentional contrast for visual interest. Consider the finish of the beads as well—matte, shiny, metallic, or iridescent finishes can all contribute to the overall look of your piece.
Pay Attention to Size and Shape:

Beads come in a variety of sizes and shapes, each offering unique design possibilities. Consider the scale of your project and choose beads that are proportionate to the overall size. Experiment with different bead shapes, such as round, oval, faceted, or irregular, to add texture and dimension to your design.
Factor in Material and Durability:

Beads are available in a wide range of materials, from natural gemstones and glass to metal, ceramic, and polymer clay. Consider the durability and suitability of the materials for your intended use. For example, if you're making earrings or bracelets that will be worn frequently, opt for durable materials like glass or metal. If your design requires lightweight beads, consider materials like acrylic or resin.
Personalize with Meaningful Elements:

Incorporate beads with personal significance or symbolic meaning into your designs to add depth and sentimentality. Birthstone beads, charms, or beads with cultural or spiritual significance can infuse your jewelry with meaning and connect with the wearer on a deeper level.
Experiment and Have Fun:

Don't be afraid to experiment with different bead combinations and techniques. Mix and match beads of varying shapes, sizes, and materials to create unique and one-of-a-kind designs. Let your creativity guide you and trust your intuition when selecting beads for your projects.

By following these guidelines and considering the project type, design style, colors, sizes, shapes, materials, and personal significance of the beads, you'll be able to select the perfect beads for your jewelry projects. Whether you're creating a simple stringing project or an elaborate beadwork design, choosing the right beads is the first step towards bringing your creative vision to life. So, let your imagination soar and enjoy the process of selecting beads that inspire and delight you!

Chapter: Wirework Wonders: Introduction to Wireworking Tools and Materials

Wireworking is a versatile and captivating technique in jewelry making, offering endless possibilities for creating intricate designs, decorative elements, and structural components. Whether you're a beginner or an experienced jewelry maker, understanding the essential tools and materials used in wireworking is key to mastering this art form. In this chapter, we'll explore the fundamental tools and materials needed for wireworking and provide guidance on how to select the right ones for your projects.

Wireworking Tools:

Round-Nose Pliers: These pliers feature rounded jaws that taper to a point, making them ideal for creating loops, curves, and bends in wire.
Chain-Nose Pliers: Also known as flat-nose pliers, these have flat, tapered jaws that are perfect for gripping, bending, and manipulating wire.
Wire Cutters: Essential for cutting wire to size, wire cutters come in various sizes and styles, including flush cutters for cutting wire close to the work surface.
Nylon Jaw Pliers: These specialized pliers feature nylon jaws that prevent scratching or marring of wire surfaces, making them ideal for straightening and shaping wire without leaving marks.

Bail-Making Pliers: These pliers have round, barrel-shaped jaws in various sizes, allowing you to create consistent loops and coils for bails, ear wires, and other wire components.
Wireworking Materials:

Wire: Wire is available in various gauges (thicknesses) and materials, including copper, sterling silver, gold-filled, brass, and stainless steel. Choose the appropriate gauge and material for your project based on its strength, flexibility, and desired finish.
Beads: Beads can be incorporated into wireworking designs to add color, texture, and visual interest. Choose beads in compatible sizes and materials that complement your wirework.
Findings: Findings such as clasps, jump rings, ear wires, and bead caps are essential for completing wirework projects and connecting components securely.
Tools and Supplies: In addition to pliers and wire cutters, other tools and supplies commonly used in wireworking include wire straighteners, mandrels, hammers, bench blocks, and shaping tools.
Selecting Wireworking Materials:

Gauge: Wire gauge refers to the thickness of the wire, with higher gauge numbers indicating thinner wire. Choose a wire gauge appropriate for your project's requirements, such as strength, durability, and flexibility. Thicker gauges are suitable for structural components and sculptural wirework, while thinner gauges are ideal for intricate designs and delicate wire wrapping.
Material: Consider the material of the wire based on its color, finish, and suitability for your project. Copper wire is popular for its affordability, malleability, and warm color tones, while precious metals like sterling silver and gold-filled wire offer durability, shine, and a luxurious finish.

Finish: Wire is available in various finishes, including bare, oxidized, plated, and enameled. Choose a finish that complements your design aesthetic and enhances the overall look of your wirework.

By familiarizing yourself with the essential tools and materials used in wireworking and understanding how to select the right ones for your projects, you'll be well-equipped to embark on your wireworking journey with confidence and creativity. Experiment with different wire gauges, materials, and techniques to discover the endless possibilities of wireworking and unleash your artistic potential. So, gather your tools and materials, and let your imagination soar as you explore the wondrous world of wireworking!

Chapter: Basic Wireworking Techniques: Step-by-Step Instructions

Wireworking is a versatile and captivating art form that allows you to create intricate designs, structural elements, and decorative accents using wire. Whether you're a beginner or looking to expand your wireworking skills, mastering basic wireworking techniques is essential for creating beautiful and professional-looking jewelry pieces. In this chapter, we'll explore step-by-step instructions for some fundamental wireworking techniques, including wire wrapping, coiling, and shaping.

Wire Wrapping:
Wire wrapping is a fundamental technique in jewelry making that involves securing beads, stones, or other components using wire. Here's how to wire wrap a bead:

Cut a length of wire approximately twice the width of the bead you want to wrap.
Grip the end of the wire with round-nose pliers and create a small loop.
Slide the bead onto the wire and position it against the loop.
Use chain-nose pliers to bend the wire at a right angle just above the bead.
Grip the wire with round-nose pliers just above the bend and wrap the wire around the pliers to form a loop.
Continue wrapping the wire around itself to form a coil, stopping when you reach the bead.

Trim any excess wire and use chain-nose pliers to tuck in the end of the wire to secure it in place.

Coiling:

Coiling is a technique used to create decorative spirals, loops, and swirls in wire. Here's how to create a simple coil:

Grip the end of the wire with round-nose pliers and create a small loop.

Hold the loop with chain-nose pliers and use your fingers to wrap the wire tightly around the loop, forming a coil.

Continue wrapping the wire around the loop until you reach the desired size of the coil.

Use wire cutters to trim any excess wire, leaving a small tail.

Use chain-nose pliers to tuck in the end of the wire to secure it in place.

Shaping:

Shaping wire allows you to create various curves, angles, and forms in your wirework designs. Here's how to shape wire using pliers:

Grip the wire with chain-nose pliers at the point where you want to create a bend.

Use your fingers or additional pliers to bend the wire to the desired angle or curve.

Adjust the position of the pliers and continue bending the wire until you achieve the desired shape.

Use round-nose pliers to create loops or curves in the wire, or to refine the shape of your design.

Hammering:

Hammering wire can add texture, strength, and visual interest to your wirework designs. Here's how to hammer wire:

Place the wire on a bench block or anvil and secure it in place with masking tape or a clamp.

Use a jewelry hammer to gently tap the wire, creating texture or flattening the surface.

Experiment with different hammering techniques and patterns to achieve the desired effect.

Be mindful not to hammer the wire too forcefully, as it may cause it to become brittle or misshapen.

By mastering these basic wireworking techniques—wire wrapping, coiling, shaping, and hammering—you'll have the skills and confidence to create a wide variety of wirework designs and jewelry pieces. Experiment with different wire gauges, materials, and techniques to explore the endless possibilities of wireworking and unleash your creativity. So, gather your tools and materials, and let your imagination soar as you embark on your wireworking journey!

Chapter: Wire Wrapping

Wire wrapping is a fundamental technique in jewelry making that allows you to securely attach beads, stones, or other components using wire. Whether you're creating earrings, pendants, or intricate wirework designs, mastering the art of wire wrapping will open up a world of creative possibilities. In this chapter, we'll explore step-by-step instructions for wire wrapping a bead, one of the most common applications of this versatile technique.

Gather Your Materials:
Before you begin wire wrapping, gather the following materials:

Bead to be wrapped
Wire (appropriate gauge for your project, such as 20 or 22 gauge)
Round-nose pliers
Chain-nose pliers
Wire cutters
Cut the Wire:

Cut a length of wire approximately twice the width of the bead you want to wrap. This will provide enough wire to create the wrapping loop and secure the bead in place.
Create a Loop:

Grip the end of the wire with round-nose pliers and create a small loop by rotating the pliers away from you. The size of the loop will depend on the desired size of your wrapped loop.
Slide the Bead onto the Wire:

Slide the bead onto the straight section of the wire and position it against the loop you created. Ensure that the loop is large enough to accommodate the bead and allow for movement.

Bend the Wire:

Use chain-nose pliers to grip the wire just above the bead and bend it at a right angle, away from the bead. This bend will help secure the bead in place and provide a starting point for wrapping.

Form the Wrapped Loop:

Grip the wire with round-nose pliers just above the bend you created. Rotate the pliers to form a loop by bringing the wire over the top jaw of the pliers and towards the bead.

Continue wrapping the wire around the pliers until it meets the beginning of the loop, forming a coil. Ensure that the coils are tight and evenly spaced for a neat finish.

Secure the Wire:

Once you've wrapped enough wire to create a secure loop, use wire cutters to trim any excess wire, leaving a small tail.

Use chain-nose pliers to tuck in the end of the wire, securing it against the coil and preventing any sharp edges.

Final Inspection:

Give your wire-wrapped bead a final inspection to ensure that the loop is securely closed, the wire is neatly wrapped, and the bead is securely attached.

Gently tug on the bead to test its stability and ensure that the wire is securely wrapped around it.

Wire wrapping allows you to create elegant and durable connections in your jewelry designs, making it an essential skill for any jewelry maker. Experiment with different wire gauges, bead sizes, and wrapping styles to create unique and personalized pieces that showcase your creativity and craftsmanship. So, gather your materials and tools, and let your imagination soar as you explore the endless possibilities of wire wrapping in your jewelry making journey!

Chapter: Coiling

Coiling is a versatile wireworking technique that adds decorative accents, texture, and dimension to your jewelry designs. By mastering the art of coiling, you can create beautiful spirals, loops, and swirls that enhance the visual appeal of your wirework creations. In this chapter, we'll explore step-by-step instructions for creating a simple coil using wire and basic wireworking tools.

Gather Your Materials:
Before you begin coiling, gather the following materials:

Wire (appropriate gauge for your project, such as 20 or 22 gauge)
Round-nose pliers
Chain-nose pliers
Wire cutters
Create a Loop:

Grip the end of the wire with round-nose pliers and create a small loop by rotating the pliers away from you. The size of the loop will depend on the desired size of your coil.
Hold the Loop and Start Coiling:

Hold the loop firmly with chain-nose pliers to stabilize it. Use your fingers to wrap the wire tightly around the loop, starting from the base of the loop and working towards the tip.
Continue Wrapping:

Continue wrapping the wire around the loop in a tight, even spiral motion. Use your fingers to guide the wire and maintain consistent spacing between each coil.
Adjust the Size and Shape:

As you coil the wire, you can adjust the size and shape of the coil by applying more or less tension to the wire and varying the spacing between coils. Experiment with different techniques to create coils of varying sizes and shapes.

Reach Desired Size:

Continue wrapping the wire around the loop until you reach the desired size of the coil. Keep in mind that you can always add more wire to the coil if needed, so focus on achieving a consistent and even coil.

Trim Excess Wire:

Once you've reached the desired size of the coil, use wire cutters to trim any excess wire, leaving a small tail. Be careful not to cut the wire too close to the coil to avoid unraveling.

Secure the Coil:

Use chain-nose pliers to tuck in the end of the wire, securing it against the coil and preventing any sharp edges. Ensure that the end of the wire is tucked securely to prevent it from coming loose.

Coiling is a versatile technique that can be used to create decorative elements, focal points, and structural components in your wirework designs. Experiment with different wire gauges, materials, and coil sizes to explore the endless possibilities of coiling in your jewelry making projects. So, gather your materials and tools, and let your creativity soar as you add beautiful coils to your wirework creations!

Chapter: Shaping

Shaping wire is a fundamental skill in wireworking that allows you to create various curves, angles, and forms in your jewelry designs. Whether you're sculpting intricate wire motifs or bending wire to fit a specific design, mastering the art of shaping wire will enhance the visual appeal and structural integrity of your creations. In this chapter, we'll explore step-by-step instructions for shaping wire using pliers and additional tools.

Gather Your Materials:
Before you begin shaping wire, gather the following materials:

Wire (appropriate gauge for your project, such as 20 or 22 gauge)
Chain-nose pliers
Round-nose pliers (optional)
Additional pliers or tools (optional)
Grip the Wire:

Grip the wire firmly with chain-nose pliers at the point where you want to create a bend or curve. Position the pliers close to the area where you want the bend to occur.
Bend the Wire:

Use your fingers or additional pliers to bend the wire to the desired angle or curve. Apply gentle pressure to the wire, gradually shaping it into the desired form.
For sharper bends or tighter curves, you may need to use additional pliers or tools to apply more force and control the shape of the wire.
Adjust the Position:

As you bend the wire, adjust the position of the pliers to ensure that the bend is smooth and even. Use the pliers to grip the wire firmly and guide it into the desired shape.

Continue Shaping.

Continue bending the wire until you achieve the desired shape for your design. Take your time and make small adjustments as needed to refine the shape and ensure symmetry.

Create Loops or Curves:

If you want to create loops or curves in the wire, use round-nose pliers to grip the wire and rotate them to form circular shapes. Experiment with different sizes of round-nose pliers to create loops of varying diameters.

Refine the Shape:

Use round-nose pliers to refine the shape of your design, adjusting the angles and curves as needed. Rotate the pliers gently to smooth out any rough edges and create a polished finish.

Final Inspection:

Give your wire shape a final inspection to ensure that it meets your design specifications. Check for symmetry, smoothness, and stability, making any final adjustments as needed. Shaping wire allows you to bring your creative visions to life, whether you're crafting intricate wire motifs, forming structural elements, or adding decorative accents to your jewelry designs. Experiment with different wire gauges, shapes, and techniques to explore the endless possibilities of shaping wire in your wireworking projects. So, gather your materials and tools, and let your imagination soar as you shape wire into beautiful designs!

Chapter: Hammering

Hammering wire is a transformative technique in wireworking that can elevate your designs by adding texture, strength, and visual interest. Whether you're aiming to create a rustic, hammered texture or flatten wire for a sleek and polished finish, mastering the art of hammering will enhance the versatility and dimensionality of your wirework creations. In this chapter, we'll explore step-by-step instructions for hammering wire and provide tips for achieving different effects.

Prepare Your Workspace:
Before you begin hammering wire, ensure you have the following materials and tools:

Wire (appropriate gauge for your project)
Bench block or anvil
Masking tape or clamps (to secure the wire)
Jewelry hammer (with a flat or textured surface)
Safety goggles (optional, but recommended)
Secure the Wire:

Place the wire on a bench block or anvil and secure it in place using masking tape or clamps. This will prevent the wire from shifting or moving while you hammer it.
Choose Your Hammer:

Select a jewelry hammer with the desired surface texture for your project. Flat-faced hammers will flatten the wire, while textured hammers will create patterns and indentations.
Hammer the Wire:

Hold the hammer with a firm grip and use a controlled, even motion to gently tap the wire. Start with light taps and gradually increase the force as needed to achieve the desired effect.

Experiment with different hammering techniques, such as tapping the wire repeatedly in one spot to create a hammered texture or moving the hammer across the wire to create a linear pattern.

Rotate the Wire:

Rotate the wire periodically as you hammer to ensure even coverage and consistent texture or pattern across the surface. This will prevent the wire from becoming misshapen or unevenly hammered.

Control the Force:

Be mindful not to hammer the wire too forcefully, as this can cause it to become brittle or misshapen. Use a controlled, moderate force to achieve the desired effect without damaging the wire.

Experiment with Patterns and Textures:

Experiment with different hammering techniques and patterns to achieve a variety of textures and visual effects. Try overlapping hammer strikes, varying the angle of the hammer, or using different parts of the hammer face to create unique patterns and indentations.

Final Inspection:

Once you've finished hammering the wire, inspect it carefully to ensure that the texture or pattern meets your design specifications. Make any final adjustments as needed to achieve the desired effect.

Hammering wire is a versatile technique that can add depth, character, and dimension to your wirework designs. Experiment with different hammering techniques, surfaces, and patterns to explore the endless possibilities of hammering in your wireworking projects. So, gather your materials and tools, and let your creativity flow as you transform plain wire into beautifully textured and embellished designs!

Chapter: Projects Incorporating Wirework

Wirework is a versatile and dynamic technique that can be incorporated into a wide range of jewelry designs, from intricate wire-wrapped pendants to delicate wirework earrings. In this chapter, we'll explore step-by-step projects that showcase the creative potential of wirework, allowing you to create stunning and unique jewelry pieces that reflect your personal style and craftsmanship.

Wire-Wrapped Pendant:

Materials Needed:
Large focal bead or gemstone
Wire (appropriate gauge for wrapping, such as 20 or 22 gauge)
Chain or cord for necklace
Instructions:
Cut a length of wire approximately four times the width of the focal bead.
Grip one end of the wire with round-nose pliers and create a small loop.
Slide the focal bead onto the wire and position it against the loop.
Use chain-nose pliers to bend the wire at a right angle just above the bead.
Grip the wire with round-nose pliers just above the bend and wrap the wire around the pliers to form a loop.
Continue wrapping the wire around itself to form a coil, stopping when you reach the bead.

Trim any excess wire and use chain-nose pliers to tuck in the end of the wire to secure it in place.

Attach a chain or cord to the loop to complete the pendant.

Wirework Earrings:

Materials Needed:

Beads or gemstones for earrings

Wire (appropriate gauge for earrings, such as 20 or 22 gauge)

Earring hooks or studs

Instructions:

Cut a length of wire approximately twice the desired length of the earring plus extra for wrapping.

Slide a bead or gemstone onto the wire and position it in the center.

Grip the wire with round-nose pliers just above the bead and bend it at a right angle.

Grip the wire with chain-nose pliers and wrap it around the base of the loop to form a coil.

Trim any excess wire and use chain-nose pliers to tuck in the end of the wire to secure it in place.

Attach the earring hook or stud to the loop to complete the earring.

These projects are just a starting point for incorporating wirework into your jewelry designs. Experiment with different wire gauges, bead sizes, and wrapping techniques to create unique and personalized pieces that reflect your creativity and skill. Whether you're a beginner or an experienced jewelry maker, wirework offers endless opportunities for exploration and innovation in your jewelry making journey. So, gather your materials and tools, and let your imagination soar as you create beautiful wirework jewelry pieces that inspire and delight!

Chapter: Metal Magic: Overview of Metals in Jewelry Making

Metals play a vital role in jewelry making, contributing not only to the aesthetic appeal of a piece but also to its durability, value, and overall quality. From timeless classics like silver and gold to versatile options like copper and brass, each metal brings its unique characteristics and charm to jewelry designs. In this chapter, we'll explore an overview of the metals commonly used in jewelry making, including their properties, characteristics, and popular applications.

Silver:

Sterling silver, composed of 92.5% pure silver and 7.5% other metals (usually copper), is one of the most popular metals used in jewelry making. Known for its brilliant luster, versatility, and affordability, sterling silver is a favorite choice for both traditional and contemporary designs. It can be polished to a high shine or oxidized to create a darkened patina, adding depth and contrast to jewelry pieces.
Gold:

Gold has been prized for its beauty and value for centuries, making it a timeless choice for fine jewelry. Available in various colors, including yellow, white, and rose gold, gold's purity is measured in karats, with 24-karat gold being the purest. Pure gold (24k) is too soft for jewelry making, so it's often alloyed with other metals like silver, copper, or palladium to increase its strength and durability. Gold jewelry can be crafted in a wide range of styles, from delicate filigree to bold statement pieces, making it a versatile and enduring choice for jewelry lovers.
Copper:

Copper is a malleable and affordable metal that adds warmth and character to jewelry designs. Known for its rich reddish-brown hue, copper develops a natural patina over time, adding a rustic and aged look to jewelry pieces. It's often used in combination with other metals or as a base metal for plating with silver or gold. Copper jewelry can be polished to restore its shine or left untreated to embrace its natural patina, making it a versatile and environmentally friendly option for eco-conscious jewelry makers.
Brass:

Brass is an alloy of copper and zinc, prized for its golden color, durability, and affordability. It's commonly used in jewelry making for its versatility and ability to mimic the appearance of gold at a fraction of the cost. Brass jewelry can be polished to a high shine, oxidized for an antique finish, or textured and patinated to create unique and artistic designs. It's often used as a base metal for plating with gold or silver, adding depth and dimension to jewelry pieces.
Platinum:

Platinum is a rare and precious metal valued for its strength, durability, and purity. It's naturally white in color and highly resistant to tarnish, making it an ideal choice for engagement rings, wedding bands, and heirloom-quality jewelry. Platinum jewelry is hypoallergenic and often alloyed with other platinum group metals like palladium, iridium, or ruthenium to enhance its strength and workability. While platinum jewelry is more expensive than gold or silver, its timeless elegance and longevity make it a cherished investment for generations to come.

Understanding the properties and characteristics of different metals is essential for jewelry makers to choose the right materials for their designs. Whether you prefer the classic elegance of silver and gold or the rustic charm of copper and brass, each metal offers its unique allure and endless possibilities for creativity in jewelry making. So, embrace the magic of metals and let your imagination soar as you create stunning and distinctive jewelry pieces that captivate and inspire!

Chapter: Silver

Silver, especially in the form of sterling silver, holds a special place in the world of jewelry making. Renowned for its timeless elegance, brilliant luster, and versatility, sterling silver is a beloved metal among jewelry artisans and enthusiasts alike. In this chapter, we'll delve deeper into the allure of sterling silver, exploring its composition, characteristics, and popular applications in jewelry making.

Composition and Properties:

Sterling silver is composed of 92.5% pure silver and 7.5% other metals, typically copper. This alloy is used to enhance the durability and workability of the silver, as pure silver (100%) is too soft for practical use in jewelry.
The addition of copper to silver creates a more robust metal that retains the desirable qualities of silver while improving its strength and resilience.
Sterling silver is renowned for its brilliant luster, which lends a timeless elegance to jewelry pieces. Its bright white color provides a striking contrast against gemstones and other materials, making it a versatile choice for a wide range of designs.
Versatility and Affordability:

One of the key advantages of sterling silver is its versatility. It can be fashioned into intricate filigree designs, sleek minimalist styles, or bold statement pieces, catering to a diverse range of tastes and preferences.

Sterling silver jewelry can be polished to a high shine, showcasing its reflective surface, and enhancing its visual appeal. Alternatively, it can be oxidized to create a darkened patina, adding depth and contrast to the metal, and highlighting intricate details.

Despite its luxurious appearance, sterling silver remains relatively affordable compared to other precious metals like gold or platinum, making it accessible to a wide audience of jewelry enthusiasts.

Applications in Jewelry Making:

Sterling silver is a favorite choice for both traditional and contemporary jewelry designs. It is commonly used to create earrings, necklaces, bracelets, rings, and other accessories, ranging from everyday staples to special occasion pieces. Jewelry makers appreciate sterling silver for its malleability, allowing them to create intricate details and delicate textures in their designs. It can be hammered, stamped, engraved, and soldered to achieve a variety of artistic effects.

Sterling silver provides an excellent backdrop for showcasing gemstones, pearls, and other materials. Its neutral color complements a wide range of hues, allowing gemstones to take center stage while adding a touch of elegance and sophistication to the overall design.

In conclusion, sterling silver holds a special allure in the world of jewelry making, thanks to its brilliant luster, versatility, and affordability. Whether fashioned into classic pieces or contemporary designs, sterling silver jewelry exudes timeless elegance and charm. Its ability to adapt to various styles and techniques makes it a beloved metal among jewelry artisans and a cherished choice for jewelry enthusiasts around the globe. So, embrace the beauty of sterling silver and let your creativity shine as you craft stunning and memorable jewelry pieces that captivate and inspire.

Chapter: Gold: A Timeless Treasure in Jewelry Making

Gold holds a revered status in the world of jewelry making, revered for its enduring beauty, intrinsic value, and timeless allure. For centuries, gold has been cherished as a symbol of wealth, luxury, and prestige, adorning royalty, nobility, and discerning individuals around the world. In this chapter, we'll explore the captivating qualities of gold, its diverse varieties, and its esteemed place in the realm of fine jewelry.

Composition and Varieties:

Gold's purity is measured in karats, with 24-karat gold being the purest form. Pure gold (24k) is exceptionally soft and malleable, making it unsuitable for practical use in jewelry. To enhance its durability and strength, gold is often alloyed with other metals such as silver, copper, or palladium. The addition of these alloys results in various shades of gold and different karat compositions.

Yellow gold, prized for its warm, rich hue, remains a classic choice for traditional and vintage-inspired jewelry designs. White gold, alloyed with white metals such as nickel or palladium, offers a contemporary alternative with a sleek, modern appearance. Rose gold, crafted by blending gold with copper, exudes a romantic, rosy tint that adds a touch of warmth and femininity to jewelry pieces.

Versatility and Craftsmanship:

Gold's versatility in jewelry making knows no bounds. It can be fashioned into intricate filigree patterns, sleek minimalist styles, or bold statement pieces, catering to a wide spectrum of tastes and preferences.

The malleability of gold allows skilled artisans to sculpt and shape it with precision, creating exquisite details and refined textures in their designs. From delicate engravings to elaborate settings, gold jewelry reflects the artistry and craftsmanship of its makers.

Gold's enduring appeal lies in its ability to transcend trends and fads, remaining a cherished choice for jewelry lovers across generations. Whether adorning a simple wedding band or an elaborate necklace, gold jewelry exudes an aura of elegance, sophistication, and timelessness.

Symbolism and Significance:

Gold holds profound symbolic significance in various cultures and traditions, representing wealth, prosperity, and abundance. It symbolizes enduring love and commitment in the form of wedding bands and engagement rings, serving as tangible reminders of cherished relationships and milestones. Beyond its material value, gold carries emotional resonance and sentimental meaning for many individuals. Passed down through generations as heirlooms and family treasures, gold jewelry holds stories, memories, and connections that transcend time and place.

In conclusion, gold stands as a beacon of beauty, value, and tradition in the realm of fine jewelry. Its radiant glow, inherent elegance, and timeless allure captivate hearts and inspire awe, making it a treasured choice for discerning jewelry connoisseurs worldwide. Whether crafted into classic designs or innovative creations, gold jewelry embodies the essence of luxury, sophistication, and enduring style. So, embrace the enchantment of gold and let its shimmering brilliance adorn your life with timeless elegance and grace.

Chapter: Copper: Embracing Warmth and Character in Jewelry Making

Copper, with its rich reddish-brown hue and unique characteristics, offers jewelry makers a versatile and distinctive medium to express creativity and style. Renowned for its warmth, malleability, and affordability, copper has long been prized for its ability to add depth and character to jewelry designs. In this chapter, we'll explore the enduring appeal of copper, its distinctive properties, and its diverse applications in jewelry making.

Properties and Characteristics:

Copper is a malleable metal renowned for its distinctive reddish-brown color and inherent warmth. Its softness and ductility make it an ideal material for shaping and forming into intricate designs and textures.

Over time, copper develops a natural patina as it reacts with air, moisture, and skin oils. This patina adds depth and dimension to copper jewelry, imbuing it with a rustic and aged appearance that enhances its charm and character.

Copper's affordability makes it an accessible choice for jewelry makers of all skill levels, offering a cost-effective alternative to precious metals like gold and silver. Its unique aesthetic appeal and versatility make it a popular choice for both traditional and contemporary jewelry designs.

Applications in Jewelry Making:

Copper jewelry can be crafted in a wide range of styles, from minimalist earrings to bold statement necklaces, offering endless opportunities for creativity and expression. Its warm, earthy tones complement a variety of gemstones, beads, and other materials, allowing for striking and harmonious compositions.

Copper is often used in combination with other metals such as brass or silver to create mixed-metal designs that showcase the unique properties of each material. It can also be plated with silver or gold to enhance its appearance and durability while maintaining its distinctive color and patina.

Jewelry makers appreciate copper for its eco-friendly properties, as it is a highly recyclable metal with minimal environmental impact. Its natural patina and ability to age gracefully over time add to its appeal as a sustainable and environmentally conscious choice for eco-conscious consumers.

Care and Maintenance:

Copper jewelry can be polished to restore its shine and luster using a polishing cloth or jewelry cleaner specifically formulated for copper. Alternatively, some individuals choose to embrace the natural patina that develops on copper over time, adding to its character and charm.

To prevent tarnishing and maintain the appearance of copper jewelry, store it in a cool, dry place away from direct sunlight and moisture. Avoid exposing copper jewelry to harsh chemicals, perfumes, or lotions, as these may accelerate tarnishing and dull its shine.

In conclusion, copper's warm, earthy tones and unique characteristics make it a beloved choice for jewelry makers seeking to imbue their designs with depth, warmth, and character. Whether used alone or in combination with other metals, copper jewelry exudes a timeless charm and rustic elegance that captivates the senses and delights the soul. So, embrace the allure of copper and let its radiant beauty adorn your life with warmth, style, and enduring appeal.

Chapter: Brass: A Versatile Alloy in Jewelry Making

Brass, with its radiant golden hue and remarkable versatility, stands as a beloved metal in the realm of jewelry making. Composed of copper and zinc, this alloy boasts a timeless allure, combining the warmth of copper with the brilliance of gold. In this chapter, we'll delve into the captivating qualities of brass, its diverse applications, and its enduring appeal in jewelry design.

Composition and Properties:

Brass is an alloy consisting primarily of copper and zinc, with varying proportions of each metal determining its color, hardness, and other properties. The addition of zinc to copper imbues brass with its distinctive golden color and enhances its strength and durability.

Known for its lustrous appearance and inherent warmth, brass exudes a radiant glow that evokes the elegance and sophistication of gold. Its versatility and affordability make it a popular choice for both traditional and contemporary jewelry designs.

Applications in Jewelry Making:

Brass jewelry can be crafted in a wide array of styles, from classic to modern, offering endless possibilities for creativity and expression. Its golden hue complements a variety of gemstones, beads, and other materials, allowing for striking and harmonious compositions.

Jewelry makers often utilize brass as a base metal for plating with gold or silver, creating pieces that mimic the appearance of precious metals at a fraction of the cost. This allows for the creation of luxurious-looking jewelry pieces that are accessible to a wider audience.

Brass jewelry can be polished to a high shine, revealing its radiant golden surface, and enhancing its visual appeal. Alternatively, it can be oxidized or treated to create an antique finish, adding depth and character to the metal, and highlighting intricate details.

Versatility and Artistry:

Brass's malleability and ductility make it an ideal material for shaping and forming into intricate designs and textures. It can be stamped, engraved, textured, or patinated to create unique and artistic effects, showcasing the creativity and skill of the artisan.

Brass jewelry exudes a timeless charm and elegance that transcends trends and fads, making it a cherished choice for jewelry enthusiasts of all ages. Whether adorning a simple pendant or an elaborate statement piece, brass jewelry radiates a sense of style, sophistication, and enduring beauty.

Care and Maintenance:

To maintain the appearance of brass jewelry, it's important to clean it regularly using a soft polishing cloth or jewelry cleaner specifically formulated for brass. Avoid using abrasive cleaners or harsh chemicals, as these may damage the metal or remove its protective finish.

Store brass jewelry in a cool, dry place away from direct sunlight and moisture to prevent tarnishing and discoloration. Consider storing it in a jewelry box or pouch to protect it from scratches and abrasions when not in use.

In conclusion, brass's radiant beauty, versatility, and affordability make it a cherished metal in the world of jewelry making. Whether fashioned into classic designs or innovative creations, brass jewelry exudes timeless elegance and style, captivating hearts, and inspiring imaginations. So, embrace the allure of brass and let its golden glow adorn your life with warmth, sophistication, and enduring beauty.

Chapter: Platinum: The Epitome of Elegance and Endurance

Platinum, revered for its rarity, purity, and unparalleled beauty, stands as the epitome of luxury and sophistication in the world of jewelry making. With its naturally white color, exceptional strength, and resistance to tarnish, platinum has long been prized for creating exquisite pieces of jewelry that transcend time and trends. In this chapter, we'll delve into the extraordinary qualities of platinum, its significance in jewelry design, and its enduring appeal as a symbol of enduring love and refinement.

Composition and Properties:

Platinum is a naturally occurring metal that belongs to the platinum group of metals, which also includes palladium, iridium, and ruthenium. It is renowned for its remarkable purity, durability, and resistance to corrosion, making it an ideal choice for crafting heirloom-quality jewelry.
Unlike other precious metals such as gold or silver, platinum is naturally white in color, possessing a luminous and enduring brilliance that sets it apart. Its cool, silvery hue serves as a stunning backdrop for showcasing the brilliance of diamonds and other gemstones, creating a timeless and elegant aesthetic.
Platinum jewelry is hypoallergenic, making it an excellent choice for individuals with sensitive skin. Its purity and inertness ensure that it does not react with the skin, reducing the risk of allergic reactions or irritation commonly associated with other metals.
Applications in Jewelry Making:

Platinum's exceptional durability and resistance to wear make it an ideal choice for crafting engagement rings, wedding bands, and other pieces of jewelry that are meant to be worn daily and cherished for a lifetime. Its strength allows for intricate and delicate designs that retain their beauty and integrity over time.

Platinum jewelry is often alloyed with other platinum group metals such as palladium, iridium, or ruthenium to enhance its strength, durability, and workability. These alloys provide additional hardness and resilience while maintaining the metal's inherent purity and brilliance.

Platinum's timeless elegance and understated luxury make it a coveted choice for both classic and contemporary jewelry designs. From sleek solitaire engagement rings to intricately embellished bracelets, platinum jewelry exudes sophistication, refinement, and enduring beauty.

Investment and Significance:

While platinum jewelry may be more expensive than gold or silver, its exceptional durability, longevity, and intrinsic value make it a cherished investment for generations to come. Platinum jewelry retains its beauty and luster indefinitely, making it a symbol of enduring love, commitment, and refinement.

Platinum's rarity and purity make it a symbol of exclusivity and prestige, coveted by discerning individuals who appreciate its inherent beauty and timeless allure. Its enduring appeal transcends fleeting trends and fads, ensuring that platinum jewelry remains a treasured possession and a testament to lasting love and sophistication.

In conclusion, platinum stands as a paragon of elegance, endurance, and refinement in the world of jewelry making. Its timeless beauty, exceptional durability, and symbolic significance make it a cherished choice for celebrating life's most meaningful moments. Whether adorning an engagement ring, wedding band, or heirloom-quality piece, platinum jewelry embodies the essence of enduring love, sophistication, and timeless elegance. So, embrace the allure of platinum and let its luminous beauty adorn your life with grace, refinement, and eternal enchantment.

Chapter: Introduction to Metalworking Tools and Safety Precautions

Metalworking is a captivating craft that allows artisans to transform raw materials into exquisite jewelry pieces through a combination of skill, creativity, and precision. Whether you're a seasoned metalsmith or a novice jeweler eager to explore the art of metalworking, understanding the essential tools and safety precautions is crucial for a successful and enjoyable experience. In this chapter, we'll embark on a journey into the world of metalworking tools and safety measures, equipping you with the knowledge and confidence to unleash your creativity while prioritizing your well-being.

Essential Metalworking Tools:

Jeweler's Saw: A jeweler's saw is a versatile tool used for cutting metal sheets, wires, and tubing with precision and accuracy. It consists of a thin, flexible blade attached to a frame, allowing jewelers to create intricate shapes and designs.

Bench Pin: A bench pin is a small wooden or metal platform attached to the edge of a workbench. It provides support and stability while sawing, filing, and sanding metal pieces, allowing for greater control and accuracy.

Files: Files are essential for shaping, smoothing, and refining metal surfaces. Available in various shapes and sizes, including flat, round, and half-round, files are used to remove excess metal, refine edges, and create smooth contours in jewelry pieces.

Pliers: Pliers are indispensable for bending, shaping, and securing metal components. They come in a variety of types, including chain-nose, round-nose, flat-nose, and needle-nose pliers, each designed for specific tasks such as forming loops, gripping wires, and closing jump rings.

Soldering Torch: A soldering torch is used for joining metal components together using solder. It produces a concentrated flame that heats the metal to the melting point of the solder, creating strong and durable bonds.

Mandrels: Mandrels are cylindrical tools used for shaping and sizing metal rings, bracelets, and other curved components. They come in various sizes and materials, including steel, plastic, and wood, and are essential for achieving accurate and uniform shapes.

Safety Equipment: Safety goggles, gloves, and aprons are essential for protecting yourself from potential hazards such as flying debris, hot metals, and chemical splashes. Wearing appropriate safety gear ensures your well-being and minimizes the risk of accidents or injuries.

Safety Precautions:

Ventilation: Ensure adequate ventilation in your workspace to dissipate fumes and gases produced during soldering and metalworking processes. Work near an open window or use a ventilation hood to remove airborne contaminants and maintain a safe working environment.

Fire Safety: Keep a fire extinguisher nearby and familiarize yourself with its operation in case of emergencies. Avoid working near flammable materials and always extinguish the torch flame when not in use to prevent accidental fires.

Eye Protection: Wear safety goggles to protect your eyes from flying debris, sparks, and chemicals. Metalworking processes can generate particles and projectiles that pose a risk of eye injury, so it's essential to prioritize eye safety at all times.

Heat Protection: Use heat-resistant gloves and aprons to protect your skin from burns and injuries when handling hot metals and soldering equipment. Avoid touching hot surfaces or molten metals and exercise caution when working with open flames.

Chemical Safety: Handle chemicals such as fluxes, pickling solutions, and cleaning agents with care, following manufacturer instructions and safety guidelines. Wear gloves and work in a well-ventilated area to minimize exposure to potentially harmful substances.

By familiarizing yourself with essential metalworking tools and safety precautions, you'll be well-equipped to embark on your journey into the captivating world of jewelry making. Remember to prioritize safety at all times and approach each project with patience, precision, and creativity. With practice and dedication, you'll develop the skills and confidence to bring your metalworking visions to life, creating stunning and timeless jewelry pieces that reflect your unique style and passion.

Chapter: Basic Metalworking Techniques: A Step-by-Step Guide

Metalworking encompasses a wide range of techniques that allow artisans to shape, manipulate, and transform metal into intricate and stunning jewelry pieces. Whether you're a novice jeweler eager to explore the art of metalworking or an experienced metalsmith seeking to refine your skills, mastering basic techniques is essential for creating jewelry with precision and finesse. In this chapter, we'll embark on a journey into the world of metalworking, exploring step-by-step instructions for essential techniques such as soldering, texturing, and more.

Soldering:
Soldering is a fundamental technique used to join metal components together using solder, a low-melting-point alloy. Follow these steps for successful soldering:

a. Prepare the surfaces to be joined by cleaning them with a wire brush or abrasive pad to remove dirt, oxides, and other contaminants.
b. Apply flux to the cleaned surfaces to prevent oxidation and promote solder flow.
c. Position the metal components in alignment and secure them using binding wire or tweezers.
d. Heat the metal components evenly using a soldering torch until they reach the melting point of the solder.
e. Touch the solder to the joint, allowing it to flow into the gap between the metal components.

f. Remove the heat source and allow the solder to cool and solidify, forming a strong and durable bond.

Texturing:
Texturing is a technique used to add visual interest and dimension to metal surfaces. Follow these steps to texture metal:

a. Choose a texturing tool or method, such as hammering, stamping, or rolling with a texture plate.
b. Secure the metal sheet or component in place using a bench vise or clamps to prevent movement.
c. Apply even pressure to the metal surface using the selected texturing tool, creating patterns, indentations, or textures.
d. Experiment with different texturing techniques and tools to achieve desired effects, such as hammered, stippled, or embossed textures.
e. Refine and polish the textured surface as needed, using abrasive pads or polishing compounds to highlight the texture and remove any rough edges.

Forming:
Forming is a technique used to shape metal into three-dimensional forms, such as rings, bracelets, or earrings. Follow these steps for basic metal forming:

a. Choose a forming tool or method, such as bending, folding, dapping, or raising.
b. Secure the metal sheet or component in place using a bench vise or forming block to provide support and stability.
c. Use pliers, hammers, mandrels, or forming stakes to bend, shape, or manipulate the metal into desired forms and contours.
d. Apply gradual pressure and work methodically to avoid creating stress or distortion in the metal.

e. Fine-tune the shape and proportions as needed, ensuring symmetry and balance in the final design.

Piercing and Sawing:
Piercing and sawing are techniques used to cut metal sheets or components into desired shapes and patterns. Follow these steps for piercing and sawing:

a. Transfer the design or pattern onto the metal surface using a scribe, marker, or template.
b. Secure the metal sheet or component in place using a bench vise or clamps to prevent movement.
c. Select a jeweler's saw with an appropriate blade size and tension for the desired cutting action.
d. Begin sawing along the marked lines, applying gentle pressure, and using a fluid, back-and-forth motion to cut through the metal.
e. Rotate the metal sheet or reposition the saw as needed to follow curves, corners, and intricate details.
f. Use files or sandpaper to smooth and refine the edges of the cut metal, removing any burrs or rough spots.

By mastering these basic metalworking techniques — soldering, texturing, forming, piercing, and sawing — you'll have the skills and confidence to embark on your journey into the captivating world of jewelry making. Remember to practice patience, precision, and creativity as you explore these techniques, and don't hesitate to experiment and push the boundaries of your craft. With dedication and perseverance, you'll unlock the full potential of metalworking, creating stunning and timeless jewelry pieces that reflect your unique style and passion.

Chapter: Soldering: Joining Metals with Precision and Strength

Soldering is a foundational technique in metalworking that allows artisans to join metal components together with precision and strength. Whether you're assembling intricate jewelry pieces or crafting structural elements, mastering the art of soldering is essential for achieving professional-quality results. In this chapter, we'll explore the step-by-step process of soldering, equipping you with the knowledge and skills to create seamless and durable bonds in your metalwork projects.

Step-by-Step Instructions for Soldering:

Prepare the Surfaces:
Begin by cleaning the surfaces to be joined using a wire brush or abrasive pad to remove dirt, oxides, and other contaminants. Proper surface preparation is essential for ensuring a strong and reliable bond.
Apply Flux:
Apply flux to the cleaned surfaces to prevent oxidation and promote solder flow. Flux serves as a barrier between the metal and the atmosphere, preventing the formation of oxides that can interfere with the soldering process.
Position the Components:

Position the metal components to be soldered in alignment and secure them in place using binding wire, tweezers, or third-hand tools. Proper alignment ensures that the solder flows evenly and creates a seamless bond between the metal surfaces.

Heat the Components:
Using a soldering torch or flame, heat the metal components evenly until they reach the melting point of the solder. Apply the heat gradually and evenly to avoid overheating or warping the metal.

Apply Solder:
Once the metal components are heated sufficiently, touch the solder to the joint, allowing it to flow into the gap between the metal surfaces. The solder should melt and spread evenly, creating a strong and durable bond.

Remove Heat and Allow Cooling:
Once the solder has flowed evenly and formed a complete bond between the metal components, remove the heat source and allow the solder to cool and solidify. Avoid disturbing the joint while it cools to ensure a seamless and durable bond.

Tips for Successful Soldering:

Use the appropriate type and size of solder for your project, taking into account the metal composition and desired strength of the bond.

Practice proper heat control and torch manipulation to avoid overheating or damaging the metal components.

Maintain a clean and well-ventilated workspace to ensure optimal soldering conditions and minimize the risk of accidents or injuries.

Practice soldering techniques on scrap metal or practice pieces before attempting to solder your final project to build confidence and proficiency.

By following these step-by-step instructions and practicing proper soldering techniques, you'll be able to create seamless and durable bonds in your metalworking projects with confidence and precision. Whether you're assembling intricate jewelry pieces or fabricating structural elements, mastering the art of soldering opens up a world of creative possibilities and allows you to bring your metalwork visions to life with skill and finesse.

Chapter: Texturing: Adding Depth and Dimension to Metal Surfaces

Texturing is a versatile technique in metalworking that allows artisans to imbue metal surfaces with visual interest, depth, and character. Whether you're crafting jewelry, decorative objects, or architectural elements, mastering the art of texturing opens up a world of creative possibilities and allows you to infuse your metalwork projects with unique and captivating textures. In this chapter, we'll explore the step-by-step process of texturing metal, guiding you through the methods and techniques to achieve stunning textured effects.

Step-by-Step Instructions for Texturing Metal:

Choose a Texturing Method:
Begin by selecting a texturing method or tool that suits your project and desired aesthetic. Common texturing techniques include hammering, stamping, rolling with a texture plate, or using specialized texturing hammers or punches.
Secure the Metal:

Secure the metal sheet or component in place using a bench vise, clamps, or a sturdy work surface to prevent movement during texturing. Ensuring stability is essential for achieving uniform and consistent textures.

Apply Even Pressure:

With the metal securely in place, apply even pressure to the surface using the selected texturing tool. Experiment with different pressure levels and angles to create patterns, indentations, or textures that enhance the visual appeal of the metal.

Explore Different Techniques:

Experiment with various texturing techniques and tools to achieve different effects and textures. Whether you prefer hammered, stippled, embossed, or etched textures, exploring different methods allows you to discover unique and captivating textures that elevate your metalwork projects.

Refine and Polish:

After texturing, refine and polish the textured surface as needed to highlight the texture and remove any rough edges. Use abrasive pads, sandpaper, or polishing compounds to smooth the surface and bring out the full beauty of the texture.

Tips for Successful Texturing:

Start with a clean and smooth metal surface to ensure optimal results when texturing.

Experiment with different texturing tools, techniques, and patterns to discover unique textures and effects.

Practice on scrap metal or practice pieces to familiarize yourself with different texturing methods and refine your skills.

Consider combining texturing techniques with other metalworking techniques, such as soldering or patination, to create multidimensional and visually captivating effects.

By following these step-by-step instructions and experimenting with different texturing techniques, you'll be able to infuse your metalwork projects with depth, dimension, and visual interest. Whether you're embellishing jewelry pieces, creating decorative objects, or fabricating architectural elements, mastering the art of texturing allows you to unleash your creativity and bring your metalwork visions to life with stunning textured effects.

Chapter: Forming: Shaping Metal into Three-Dimensional Masterpieces

Forming is a transformative technique in metalworking that allows artisans to shape metal into three-dimensional forms, bringing their creative visions to life with depth, dimension, and elegance. Whether you're crafting delicate earrings, sculptural bracelets, or intricate rings, mastering the art of forming empowers you to create stunning metalwork pieces that captivate the senses and inspire the imagination. In this chapter, we'll explore the step-by-step process of metal forming, guiding you through the methods and techniques to shape metal into captivating works of art.

Step-by-Step Instructions for Basic Metal Forming:

Choose a Forming Method:

Begin by selecting a forming method or tool that suits your project and desired outcome. Common forming techniques include bending, folding, dapping, raising, sinking, and forging, each offering unique opportunities for shaping metal into three-dimensional forms.

Secure the Metal:

Secure the metal sheet or component in place using a bench vise, forming block, or other sturdy support to provide stability and prevent movement during forming. Ensuring a stable work surface is essential for achieving precise and consistent results.

Use Forming Tools:

Utilize a variety of forming tools, such as pliers, hammers, mandrels, or forming stakes, to bend, shape, or manipulate the metal into desired forms and contours. Experiment with different tools and techniques to achieve the desired shapes, curves, and textures.

Apply Gradual Pressure:

Apply gradual pressure and work methodically when forming the metal to avoid creating stress or distortion in the material. Take care to distribute pressure evenly and avoid excessive force, which can cause the metal to deform or become misshapen.

Fine-Tune the Shape:

Fine-tune the shape and proportions of the formed metal as needed, ensuring symmetry, balance, and alignment in the final design. Make any necessary adjustments to achieve the desired aesthetic and functional properties of the metalwork piece.

Tips for Successful Metal Forming:

Choose the appropriate forming method and tools based on the desired outcome and complexity of the project.
Practice proper technique and precision when manipulating the metal to achieve smooth, uniform, and symmetrical forms.

Experiment with different metals, thicknesses, and finishes to explore the unique properties and possibilities of each material.

Take breaks and assess your progress periodically to ensure that the metalwork piece is evolving according to your vision and specifications.

By following these step-by-step instructions and incorporating best practices for metal forming, you'll be able to shape metal into three-dimensional masterpieces that showcase your creativity, skill, and artistic vision. Whether you're crafting jewelry, sculptures, or functional objects, mastering the art of forming opens up a world of creative possibilities and allows you to transform raw materials into captivating works of art that delight and inspire.

Chapter: Piercing and Sawing: Precision Cutting for Intricate Designs

Piercing and sawing are essential techniques in metalworking that allow artisans to cut metal sheets or components into desired shapes and patterns with precision and accuracy. Whether you're crafting intricate filigree designs, delicate components, or custom metalwork pieces, mastering the art of piercing and sawing empowers you to bring your creative visions to life with impeccable detail and craftsmanship. In this chapter, we'll delve into the step-by-step process of piercing and sawing, guiding you through the methods and techniques to achieve flawless cuts and intricate patterns in metalwork.

Step-by-Step Instructions for Piercing and Sawing:

Transfer the Design:
Begin by transferring the design or pattern onto the metal surface using a scribe, marker, or template. Take care to mark the lines accurately, ensuring that they align with your desired shape and dimensions.
Secure the Metal:
Secure the metal sheet or component in place using a bench vise, clamps, or a sturdy work surface to prevent movement during piercing and sawing. Ensuring stability is crucial for achieving precise cuts and maintaining control over the cutting process.
Select the Saw and Blade:

Choose a jeweler's saw with an appropriate blade size and tension for the desired cutting action. Select a fine-toothed blade for intricate designs and tight curves, and ensure that the blade is properly tensioned to prevent bending or breaking during cutting.

Begin Sawing:

Start sawing along the marked lines, applying gentle pressure and using a fluid, back-and-forth motion to cut through the metal. Keep the saw blade perpendicular to the metal surface and maintain a steady pace to achieve clean and accurate cuts.

Navigate Curves and Details:

Rotate the metal sheet or reposition the saw as needed to follow curves, corners, and intricate details in the design. Take your time and exercise patience, adjusting the angle and direction of the saw to navigate tight curves and achieve precise cuts.

Refine the Edges:

After completing the cuts, use files or sandpaper to smooth and refine the edges of the cut metal, removing any burrs or rough spots. Take care to file evenly and gently to avoid distorting the shape or dimensions of the pierced metal.

Tips for Successful Piercing and Sawing:

Choose a saw blade with the appropriate size and tooth count for the thickness and type of metal you're cutting.

Practice proper sawing technique, maintaining a steady hand and consistent pressure to achieve smooth and even cuts.

Start with simple designs and gradually progress to more intricate patterns as you gain confidence and proficiency in piercing and sawing.

Use lubricants such as beeswax or cutting oil to reduce friction and prolong the life of the saw blade during cutting.

By following these step-by-step instructions and incorporating best practices for piercing and sawing, you'll be able to cut metal with precision and finesse, creating intricate designs and patterns that elevate your metalwork projects to new heights of craftsmanship and creativity. Whether you're crafting jewelry, decorative objects, or custom metalwork pieces, mastering the art of piercing and sawing allows you to unleash your creativity and bring your artistic visions to life with impeccable detail and precision.

Chapter: Metalworking Projects: Transforming Metal into Wearable Art

In this chapter, we'll explore exciting metalworking projects that showcase various techniques such as stamping, piercing, sawing, and hammering. These projects are designed to inspire creativity and provide opportunities for artisans to experiment with different metalworking techniques while creating stunning jewelry pieces.

Stamped Bracelets:

Create personalized and unique stamped bracelets by combining metal stamping with forming techniques. Start by selecting a metal sheet of your choice and cutting it into bracelet blanks using a jeweler's saw. Next, design and transfer your desired pattern onto the metal surface using metal stamps and a hammer. Experiment with different stamp designs, fonts, and textures to create custom messages, motifs, or geometric patterns. Once stamped, form the metal blanks into cuff or bangle bracelets using shaping tools such as mandrels, forming blocks, or bracelet mandrels. Finish by polishing and adding a patina or surface treatment to enhance the stamped design and give the bracelets a professional finish.

Hammered Rings:

Explore the art of hammering and shaping metal to create one-of-a-kind hammered rings with unique textures and organic shapes. Begin by selecting a metal wire or sheet of the desired gauge and composition for your rings. Cut the metal into ring blanks using a jeweler's saw or metal shears, and file the edges to remove any burrs or rough spots. Next, use a jeweler's hammer to texture the surface of the metal, creating hammered patterns, textures, or designs. Experiment with different hammering techniques and patterns to achieve the desired aesthetic, from subtle dimpling to bold surface textures. Once hammered, form the metal blanks into ring shapes using mandrels, ring sizers, or ring bending pliers. Finish by polishing and buffing the rings to bring out the luster and shine of the metal, and add any desired surface treatments or embellishments to customize the rings to your style and preferences.

These projects are just a glimpse into the endless possibilities of metalworking, offering artisans the opportunity to explore their creativity and craftsmanship while creating beautiful and wearable art. Whether you're drawn to the precision of stamping, the organic textures of hammering, or the intricate designs of piercing and sawing, there's something for everyone to enjoy in the world of metalworking. So, gather your tools, materials, and inspiration, and let your imagination soar as you embark on your metalworking journey, creating stunning jewelry pieces that reflect your unique style and passion.

Chapter: Stamped Bracelets: Personalized Wearable Art

Stamped bracelets offer a wonderful opportunity to infuse your personal style and creativity into wearable art pieces. Combining the art of metal stamping with forming techniques allows you to create personalized and unique bracelets that reflect your individuality and make a statement. In this chapter, we'll explore the step-by-step process of creating stamped bracelets, from selecting materials to adding the finishing touches.

Material Selection:

Begin by selecting a metal sheet of your choice for the bracelets. Common metals used for stamped jewelry include aluminum, brass, copper, and sterling silver. Choose a metal that suits your design aesthetic, budget, and desired finish. Ensure that the metal sheet is of sufficient thickness to withstand stamping and forming without warping or distorting.

Cutting Bracelet Blanks:

Use a jeweler's saw or metal shears to cut the metal sheet into bracelet blanks of the desired size and shape. Consider the width and length of the bracelets, as well as any specific design elements or features you wish to incorporate. File the edges of the bracelet blanks to remove any sharp edges or burrs.

Design Transfer:

Design and transfer your desired pattern onto the metal surface using metal stamps and a hammer. Arrange the stamps on the metal blank to create custom messages, motifs, or geometric patterns. Experiment with different stamp designs, fonts, and textures to achieve the desired look. Use a scribe or marker to outline the design before stamping to ensure accurate placement.

Stamping Process:

Place the metal blank on a sturdy surface, such as a steel bench block or anvil, to provide support and stability during stamping. Hold the metal stamp firmly in place with one hand while striking it firmly and evenly with a hammer using the other hand. Apply consistent pressure to create clean and legible impressions. Repeat the stamping process for each design element or letter in your pattern.

Forming the Bracelets:

Once stamped, form the metal blanks into cuff or bangle bracelets using shaping tools such as mandrels, forming blocks, or bracelet mandrels. Use nylon or rubber mallets to gently shape the metal without marring or damaging the stamped design. Gradually curve the metal blanks to fit the contours of the wrist, adjusting the shape as needed for comfort and aesthetics.

Finishing Touches:

Finish the stamped bracelets by polishing the metal surface to remove any tool marks or scratches and enhance the shine. Consider adding a patina or surface treatment to highlight the stamped design and give the bracelets a professional finish. Use polishing cloths, abrasive pads, or buffing wheels to achieve the desired level of shine and luster.

Stamped bracelets offer a versatile canvas for creativity, allowing you to express yourself through personalized designs and messages. Whether you're creating a meaningful gift for a loved one or designing a statement piece for yourself, stamped bracelets are sure to make a lasting impression and spark conversation. So, gather your materials and tools, and let your imagination soar as you create stunning stamped bracelets that reflect your unique style and personality.

Chapter: Hammered Rings: Crafting Unique Metal Masterpieces

Hammered rings offer a captivating blend of rustic charm and artisanal elegance, making them sought-after jewelry pieces for those who appreciate the beauty of handcrafted design. Through the art of hammering and shaping metal, artisans can transform simple metal blanks into one-of-a-kind rings with distinctive textures and organic shapes. In this chapter, we'll delve into the step-by-step process of creating hammered rings, from material selection to final finishing touches.

Material Selection:

Begin by selecting a metal wire or sheet of the desired gauge and composition for your rings. Common metals used for hammered rings include sterling silver, copper, brass, and gold-filled wire, or sheet. Consider the color, durability, and workability of the metal when making your selection, as well as your budget and design preferences.
Cutting Ring Blanks:

Use a jeweler's saw or metal shears to cut the metal into ring blanks of the desired size and width. Determine the dimensions of the ring blanks based on your finger size and desired ring style. File the edges of the ring blanks to remove any burrs or rough spots and ensure a smooth finish.
Hammering Process:

Next, use a jeweler's hammer to texture the surface of the metal, creating hammered patterns, textures, or designs. Place the metal blank on a steel bench block or anvil to provide support and stability during hammering. Experiment with different hammering techniques and patterns to achieve the desired aesthetic, from subtle dimpling to bold surface textures. Vary the force and angle of the hammer strikes to create depth and dimension in the hammered surface.

Forming the Rings:

Once hammered, form the metal blanks into ring shapes using mandrels, ring sizers, or ring bending pliers. Place the metal blank on the appropriate-sized mandrel and use nylon or rawhide mallets to gradually shape the metal around the mandrel, adjusting the size and curvature as needed. Ensure that the ends of the metal overlap slightly to form a seamless ring band.

Finishing Touches:

Finish the hammered rings by polishing and buffing the metal surface to bring out the luster and shine. Use polishing cloths, abrasive pads, or buffing wheels to achieve a smooth and polished finish. Consider adding any desired surface treatments or embellishments, such as patinas, oxidation, or gemstone accents, to customize the rings to your style and preferences.

Hammered rings are a testament to the beauty of handcrafted design, offering a unique and personal touch to any jewelry collection. Whether you're creating a statement piece for yourself or designing a meaningful gift for a loved one, hammered rings are sure to be cherished for their craftsmanship and individuality. So, gather your materials and tools, and let your creativity flow as you craft stunning hammered rings that reflect your unique style and passion for metalworking.

Chapter: Gemstone Glamour: Exploring the World of Precious Stones

Gemstone glamour adds an enchanting allure to jewelry, captivating the eye with vibrant colors, captivating sparkle, and mystical properties. From the fiery brilliance of diamonds to the rich hues of sapphires and emeralds, gemstones offer endless possibilities for creating breathtaking jewelry pieces that dazzle and delight. In this chapter, we'll embark on a journey through the world of precious stones, exploring the different types of gemstones and their unique properties.

Diamonds:

Diamonds are perhaps the most renowned and coveted gemstones, prized for their unparalleled brilliance, durability, and rarity. Composed of pure carbon, diamonds are formed deep within the Earth's mantle under intense heat and pressure. Known for their exceptional hardness, diamonds rank as the hardest natural substance on Earth, making them ideal for use in jewelry that withstands the test of time. Diamonds come in a variety of colors, ranging from colorless to fancy yellows, pinks, blues, and greens, with each color exhibiting its unique beauty and allure.
Rubies:

Rubies are revered for their rich red color and captivating glow, symbolizing passion, vitality, and prosperity. Belonging to the corundum family of gemstones, rubies derive their vibrant hue from the presence of chromium within the crystal structure. The most prized rubies display a deep, intense red color known as "pigeon's blood," characterized by a vivid red hue with hints of blue undertones. Rubies are prized for their exceptional hardness and brilliance, making them a popular choice for statement pieces and heirloom-quality jewelry.
Sapphires:

Sapphires are esteemed for their exquisite beauty and versatility, occurring in a spectrum of colors ranging from velvety blues to vibrant yellows, pinks, greens, and purples. Like rubies, sapphires belong to the corundum family, with the presence of trace elements such as iron, titanium, and chromium imparting their distinctive colors. Blue sapphires, in particular, are highly sought after for their intense color saturation and celestial allure, symbolizing wisdom, loyalty, and nobility. Sapphires are renowned for their exceptional hardness, second only to diamonds, making them an ideal choice for engagement rings and everyday wear.
Emeralds:

Emeralds captivate the senses with their lush green hues and mesmerizing allure, symbolizing rebirth, growth, and vitality. Belonging to the beryl family of gemstones, emeralds derive their green color from trace amounts of chromium, vanadium, and iron within the crystal lattice. Emeralds are prized for their natural beauty and inherent flaws, known as "jardin," which lend each stone its unique character and charm. While emeralds are softer than diamonds, rubies, and sapphires, they are treasured for their lush green color and striking presence in jewelry designs.
Other Gemstones:

In addition to diamonds, rubies, sapphires, and emeralds, the world of gemstones encompasses a vast array of precious and semi-precious stones, each with its unique colors, properties, and symbolism. From luminous pearls and fiery opals to vibrant amethysts, citrines, and aquamarines, gemstones offer endless possibilities for creating stunning jewelry pieces that reflect your personal style and preferences.

Gemstone glamour elevates jewelry to new heights, infusing each piece with beauty, meaning, and mystique. Whether you're drawn to the timeless elegance of diamonds, the fiery passion of rubies, or the tranquil allure of sapphires and emeralds, gemstones offer a captivating canvas for creativity and self-expression. So, immerse yourself in the enchanting world of precious stones, and let their radiant beauty inspire your next jewelry masterpiece.

Chapter: Diamonds: The Epitome of Elegance and Brilliance

Diamonds have long held a position of unrivaled prestige and allure in the world of gemstones, captivating hearts and minds with their mesmerizing sparkle and timeless beauty. In this chapter, we delve into the extraordinary world of diamonds, exploring their remarkable properties, origins, and enduring appeal.

Composition and Formation:

Diamonds are composed of pure carbon atoms arranged in a crystal lattice structure, making them one of the hardest known substances on Earth. Formed deep within the Earth's mantle billions of years ago, diamonds are created under conditions of extreme heat and pressure. Volcanic eruptions then bring these precious gems closer to the Earth's surface, where they can be mined and extracted.
Hardness and Durability:

Renowned for their exceptional hardness, diamonds rank at the top of the Mohs scale with a rating of 10, making them resistant to scratching and abrasion. This remarkable durability, combined with their innate brilliance, makes diamonds an ideal choice for engagement rings, wedding bands, and heirloom-quality jewelry that withstands the rigors of everyday wear.
Color Varieties:

While diamonds are commonly associated with colorless or white stones, they also occur naturally in a spectrum of colors, including fancy yellows, pinks, blues, and greens. The presence of trace elements such as nitrogen, boron, or hydrogen during the diamond's formation process imparts these vibrant hues. Each color variation exhibits its unique beauty and rarity, with fancy colored diamonds commanding significant attention and value in the gemstone market.
Brilliance and Fire:

One of the most captivating aspects of diamonds is their remarkable brilliance and fire, which refers to the dispersion of light into the spectral colors of the rainbow. This mesmerizing play of light results from the diamond's precise cut, which maximizes the stone's ability to reflect and refract light within its facets. The quality of a diamond's cut, along with its clarity, color, and carat weight, determines its overall beauty and value.
Symbolism and Significance:

Beyond their intrinsic beauty and physical properties, diamonds hold profound symbolism and significance in cultures around the world. Often associated with love, commitment, and eternity, diamonds have become emblematic of enduring relationships and milestones such as engagements, weddings, and anniversaries. Their timeless allure and universal appeal make diamonds a cherished and meaningful choice for commemorating life's most precious moments.

Diamonds epitomize elegance, sophistication, and everlasting beauty, captivating the imagination with their unparalleled brilliance and allure. Whether adorning a ring, necklace, or pair of earrings, diamonds add a touch of luxury and refinement to any jewelry piece, serving as timeless symbols of love, strength, and resilience. So, immerse yourself in the enchanting world of diamonds, and let their radiant beauty inspire and elevate your jewelry creations to new heights of glamour and sophistication.

Chapter: Rubies: The Gemstone of Passion and Prosperity

Rubies, with their fiery red hues and mesmerizing brilliance, hold a special place in the world of gemstones, symbolizing love, vitality, and prosperity. In this chapter, we delve into the enchanting world of rubies, exploring their unique properties, origins, and enduring allure.

Composition and Formation:

Rubies belong to the corundum family of gemstones, alongside sapphires, and are composed primarily of aluminum oxide with traces of chromium responsible for their vibrant red color. Formed deep within the Earth's crust under high pressure and temperature conditions, rubies are created through the crystallization of minerals over millions of years. Their exceptional hardness, second only to diamonds, makes rubies durable and suitable for a wide range of jewelry applications.
Color Variations:

The most coveted rubies display a rich, intense red hue known as "pigeon's blood," characterized by a vivid red color with hints of blue undertones. This highly prized coloration is rare and commands a premium in the gemstone market. However, rubies also occur in a spectrum of red shades, ranging from deep crimson to lighter pinkish-red tones. The presence of chromium impurities and the crystal's structure determine the ruby's color intensity and saturation.
Brilliance and Transparency:

Rubies exhibit exceptional brilliance and transparency, with light reflecting and refracting within the crystal lattice to create a captivating glow. The finest rubies possess a velvety sheen and a high degree of clarity, allowing light to pass through unhindered and accentuating their fiery red hues. While some rubies may contain inclusions or imperfections, these natural characteristics often add to the gemstone's charm and authenticity.

Symbolism and Significance:

Throughout history, rubies have been associated with passion, vitality, and prosperity, revered as symbols of love and good fortune. In ancient cultures, rubies were believed to possess magical properties and were worn as protective talismans against harm and misfortune. Today, rubies continue to hold deep symbolic meaning, often given as gifts to commemorate special occasions such as engagements, weddings, and anniversaries.

Jewelry Applications:

Rubies are prized for their exceptional beauty and durability, making them a popular choice for a wide range of jewelry pieces, including rings, necklaces, earrings, and bracelets. Whether set as solitaire stones or combined with diamonds and other gemstones, rubies add a touch of luxury and sophistication to any jewelry design. From classic solitaire rings to elaborate statement necklaces, rubies lend a timeless elegance and allure to jewelry pieces that are treasured for generations.

Rubies embody the essence of passion, vitality, and prosperity, captivating the heart with their vibrant red hues and radiant beauty. Whether adorning a piece of fine jewelry or cherished as a standalone gemstone, rubies serve as timeless symbols of love, strength, and good fortune. So, embrace the allure of rubies and let their fiery brilliance ignite your imagination as you explore the enchanting world of gemstone jewelry.

Chapter: Sapphires: The Essence of Elegance and Versatility

Sapphires, with their mesmerizing hues and captivating allure, stand as symbols of elegance, wisdom, and nobility in the realm of gemstones. In this chapter, we embark on a journey through the enchanting world of sapphires, exploring their diverse colors, properties, and timeless appeal.

Composition and Formation:

Sapphires, like rubies, belong to the corundum family of gemstones and are primarily composed of aluminum oxide with trace elements responsible for their various colors. While blue is the most commonly associated color with sapphires, these precious gems occur in a spectrum of hues, including yellow, pink, green, purple, and orange. The presence of elements such as iron, titanium, and chromium during the crystal's formation imbues sapphires with their distinctive colors and characteristics.

Color Varieties:

Blue sapphires are perhaps the most sought-after variety, prized for their intense color saturation and celestial allure. These gems range in shades from deep velvety blue to lighter cornflower hues, each displaying its unique beauty and charm. However, sapphires also occur in a rainbow of colors, with yellow, pink, and padparadscha (a rare pink-orange hue) being particularly coveted for their rarity and allure.

Hardness and Durability:

Renowned for their exceptional hardness, sapphires rank just below diamonds on the Mohs scale with a rating of 9, making them highly resistant to scratching and abrasion. This remarkable durability, combined with their stunning beauty, makes sapphires a popular choice for a wide range of jewelry applications, including engagement rings, earrings, pendants, and bracelets.

Symbolism and Significance:

Throughout history, sapphires have been associated with wisdom, loyalty, and nobility, revered as symbols of truth, sincerity, and virtue. In ancient cultures, sapphires were believed to possess mystical powers and were worn as protective talismans against harm and evil spirits. Today, sapphires continue to hold deep symbolic meaning, often given as gifts to celebrate anniversaries, birthdays, and other special occasions.

Jewelry Applications:

Sapphires lend themselves beautifully to a variety of jewelry designs, from classic solitaire rings to elaborate statement necklaces and earrings. Blue sapphire engagement rings, in particular, have surged in popularity, thanks to their timeless elegance and enduring symbolism of love and commitment. Whether set as center stones or accent gems, sapphires add a touch of sophistication and luxury to any jewelry piece, making them cherished heirlooms to be treasured for generations.

Sapphires embody the essence of elegance, versatility, and timeless beauty, captivating the imagination with their kaleidoscope of colors and mesmerizing allure. Whether adorning a piece of fine jewelry or cherished as a standalone gemstone, sapphires serve as timeless symbols of love, wisdom, and nobility. So, immerse yourself in the enchanting world of sapphires, and let their radiant beauty inspire and elevate your jewelry creations to new heights of glamour and sophistication.

Chapter: Emeralds: The Gemstone of Renewal and Splendor

Emeralds, with their rich green hues and captivating allure, stand as timeless symbols of renewal, growth, and vitality in the world of gemstones. In this chapter, we embark on a journey through the enchanting realm of emeralds, exploring their unique properties, origins, and enduring appeal.

Composition and Formation:

Emeralds belong to the beryl family of gemstones, alongside aquamarines and morganites, and are primarily composed of beryllium aluminum silicate. The mesmerizing green color of emeralds is attributed to trace elements such as chromium, vanadium, and iron within the crystal lattice. Formed deep within the Earth's crust under conditions of intense heat and pressure, emeralds undergo a process of crystallization over millions of years, resulting in their remarkable beauty and allure.

Color and Clarity:

The most prized emeralds display a vivid, lush green hue with a velvety or silky texture, reminiscent of fresh spring foliage. Known as "emerald green," this color is highly coveted for its depth, saturation, and vibrancy. While emeralds may contain inclusions and natural flaws known as "jardin," these imperfections are embraced as part of the stone's unique character and authenticity. In fact, the presence of jardin is often considered a hallmark of genuine emeralds, adding to their allure and mystique.

Softness and Sensitivity:

Emeralds are softer and more brittle than other popular gemstones such as diamonds, rubies, and sapphires, with a hardness rating of 7.5 to 8 on the Mohs scale. As a result, emeralds require special care and handling to prevent damage or breakage. It is recommended to avoid exposing emeralds to harsh chemicals, extreme temperatures, and sudden changes in temperature, as these factors can adversely affect the stone's integrity and appearance.

Symbolism and Significance:

Throughout history, emeralds have been revered as symbols of love, rebirth, and fertility, associated with the lush greenery of spring and the renewal of life. In ancient cultures, emeralds were believed to possess mystical powers and were worn as talismans to protect against illness, evil spirits, and misfortune. Today, emeralds continue to hold deep symbolic meaning, often given as gifts to celebrate love, prosperity, and new beginnings.

Jewelry Applications:

Emeralds lend themselves beautifully to a variety of jewelry designs, from classic solitaire rings to ornate necklaces, earrings, and bracelets. Whether set as center stones or accented with diamonds and other gemstones, emeralds add a touch of sophistication and luxury to any jewelry piece. From elegant evening wear to everyday accessories, emeralds exude a timeless elegance and allure that transcends trends and fashions.

Emeralds embody the essence of renewal, growth, and natural beauty, captivating the heart with their lush green hues and mesmerizing allure. Whether adorning a piece of fine jewelry or cherished as a standalone gemstone, emeralds serve as timeless symbols of love, vitality, and the eternal cycle of life. So, immerse yourself in the enchanting world of emeralds, and let their radiant beauty inspire and elevate your jewelry creations to new heights of splendor and sophistication.

Chapter: Other Gemstones: Exploring a World of Color and Splendor

Beyond the illustrious quartet of diamonds, rubies, sapphires, and emeralds lies a treasure trove of gemstones waiting to be discovered. In this chapter, we embark on a journey through the diverse and enchanting world of other gemstones, each possessing its unique colors, properties, and allure.

Pearls:

Pearls, the only gemstone formed within living organisms, emanate a timeless elegance and sophistication. Found in freshwater and saltwater mollusks, pearls range in color from classic white and cream to hues of pink, lavender, and black. Their luminous luster and smooth, spherical shapes make pearls a coveted choice for necklaces, earrings, and bracelets, adding a touch of grace and refinement to any ensemble.
Opals:

Opals, renowned for their kaleidoscopic play-of-color, evoke a sense of wonder and enchantment. Composed of silica spheres arranged in a three-dimensional lattice, opals exhibit a mesmerizing array of colors that shift and dance with the light. From fiery reds and oranges to tranquil blues and greens, each opal possesses its unique personality and charm, making them prized collectibles and statement pieces in jewelry designs.

Amethysts:

Amethysts, with their regal purple hues, exude a sense of royalty and mystique. Belonging to the quartz family of gemstones, amethysts derive their color from trace amounts of iron within the crystal lattice. Ranging from pale lilac to deep violet, amethysts are prized for their beauty and spiritual significance, believed to promote clarity of mind, inner peace, and spiritual growth. As February's birthstone, amethysts are often featured in rings, pendants, and earrings to commemorate birthdays and special occasions.

Citrines:

Citrines, known for their sunny yellow hues, radiate warmth, joy, and positivity. A variety of quartz, citrines range in color from pale lemon to golden orange, resembling the radiant glow of sunlight. Associated with abundance and prosperity, citrines are believed to attract wealth and success to those who wear them. Whether showcased as solitaire stones or combined with other gemstones, citrines infuse jewelry designs with a vibrant burst of color and energy.

Aquamarines:

Aquamarines, with their tranquil blue hues reminiscent of the ocean's depths, evoke feelings of serenity, clarity, and relaxation. Named for the Latin words "aqua" and "marina," meaning "water of the sea," aquamarines are prized for their clarity and brilliance. Believed to enhance communication and soothe the soul, aquamarines are often featured in rings, earrings, and necklaces, serving as talismans of serenity and protection for travelers and sailors.

Gemstones offer a kaleidoscope of colors, energies, and meanings, inviting us to explore their infinite beauty and symbolism. Whether adorning a piece of fine jewelry or cherished as standalone treasures, gemstones serve as reminders of the natural wonders and mysteries of the world around us. So, indulge your senses in the radiant splendor of other gemstones, and let their exquisite beauty inspire and elevate your jewelry creations to new heights of elegance and sophistication.

Chapter: Pearls - Nature's Timeless Elegance

Pearls, often referred to as nature's treasures, hold a unique allure that has captivated humanity for centuries. Formed within the protective shells of mollusks, pearls stand apart from other gemstones due to their organic origin and distinctive luster. In this chapter, we delve into the enchanting world of pearls, exploring their origins, varieties, and enduring appeal.

Formation and Origins:

Pearls are formed within mollusks, which include oysters, mussels, and clams, as a protective response to irritants such as parasites or debris that enter their shells. When an irritant lodges itself inside the mollusk's soft tissue, the organism secretes layers of nacre, a crystalline substance composed primarily of calcium carbonate, to coat the irritant and form a pearl. This process may take several years, resulting in pearls of varying sizes, shapes, and colors.

Varieties of Pearls:

Pearls are broadly categorized into two types: freshwater pearls and saltwater pearls. Freshwater pearls are cultivated in freshwater bodies such as lakes and rivers, while saltwater pearls are grown in oceans and seas. Within each category, pearls exhibit a wide range of colors, including white, cream, pink, lavender, and black, with variations in size, shape, and luster. Each pearl's unique characteristics are influenced by factors such as the species of mollusk, the environment in which it was cultivated, and the duration of its growth.

Luster and Surface Quality:

One of the most distinctive features of pearls is their lustrous, iridescent sheen, often referred to as "orient." This luster results from the reflection, refraction, and diffraction of light as it passes through the layers of nacre. Pearls with a high luster exhibit a radiant glow and shimmering appearance, while those with a lower luster may appear dull or chalky. In addition to luster, the surface quality of pearls is assessed based on factors such as smoothness, clarity, and the presence of blemishes or imperfections.

Jewelry Applications:

Pearls have been prized for their beauty and elegance since ancient times and continue to be a cherished choice for jewelry makers and enthusiasts alike. From classic pearl necklaces and earrings to modern, innovative designs, pearls lend a touch of grace and refinement to any ensemble. Whether showcased as solitaire pearls or combined with other gemstones and precious metals, pearls exude a timeless charm and sophistication that transcends trends and fashions.

Symbolism and Significance:

Throughout history, pearls have been associated with purity, femininity, and timeless beauty, often worn by royalty and nobility as symbols of wealth and status. In various cultures, pearls have also held symbolic significance, representing wisdom, spiritual enlightenment, and emotional healing. Today, pearls are cherished as gifts to celebrate milestones such as weddings, anniversaries, and graduations, serving as tokens of love, gratitude, and appreciation.

Pearls stand as testaments to the wonders of nature, embodying elegance, grace, and timeless beauty. Whether adorning a bride on her wedding day or adding a touch of refinement to everyday attire, pearls hold a special place in the hearts of jewelry enthusiasts worldwide. So, embrace the enchantment of pearls and let their luminous presence elevate your jewelry creations to new heights of sophistication and allure.

Chapter: Citrines - Sunshine in Gemstone Form

Citrines, with their cheerful yellow hues reminiscent of the sun's warm glow, bring a burst of energy and vitality to the world of gemstones. As a variety of quartz, citrines captivate the senses with their radiant color and uplifting presence. In this chapter, we explore the captivating beauty and symbolic significance of citrines, and their role in jewelry making.

Origin and Characteristics:

Citrines belong to the quartz family of gemstones, sharing their mineral composition with amethysts, smoky quartz, and rose quartz. The vibrant yellow color of citrines is attributed to trace amounts of iron within the crystal lattice, which range in shade from pale lemon to deep golden orange. Citrines often exhibit excellent transparency and clarity, allowing light to pass through and illuminate their radiant hues with a captivating brilliance.

Symbolism and Meaning:

Throughout history, citrines have been associated with abundance, prosperity, and success. Known as the "merchant's stone," citrines are believed to attract wealth, fortune, and business opportunities to those who wear them. In addition to their financial benefits, citrines are also associated with joy, optimism, and positive energy, making them popular choices for those seeking to manifest their goals and aspirations.

Jewelry Applications:

Citrines' vibrant color and energetic aura make them versatile gemstones for jewelry designs. Whether showcased as solitaire stones in rings, pendants, or earrings, or combined with other gemstones such as diamonds, amethysts, or peridots, citrines add a pop of color and sparkle to any ensemble. Their warm, golden hues complement a variety of metals, including sterling silver, yellow gold, and rose gold, enhancing their versatility and appeal.

Care and Maintenance:

Like all gemstones, citrines require proper care and maintenance to preserve their beauty and luster. To clean citrine jewelry, simply soak the pieces in warm, soapy water and gently scrub with a soft brush to remove dirt, oil, and debris. Avoid exposure to harsh chemicals, extreme temperatures, and abrasive materials, as these may damage the gemstone's surface or setting. Store citrine jewelry in a soft pouch or lined jewelry box to prevent scratches and tarnishing.

Spiritual and Healing Properties:

In addition to their aesthetic appeal, citrines are believed to possess metaphysical properties that promote emotional well-being and spiritual growth. Citrines are said to stimulate creativity, enhance self-confidence, and attract abundance and prosperity into one's life. They are also associated with the solar plexus chakra, which governs self-esteem, personal power, and vitality, making citrines powerful tools for manifestation and transformation.

Citrines, with their radiant warmth and joyful energy, inspire optimism, creativity, and abundance in all aspects of life. Whether worn as talismans for success and prosperity or cherished for their inherent beauty and charm, citrines continue to captivate hearts and minds around the world. So, embrace the sunshine in gemstone form and let the golden glow of citrines illuminate your jewelry creations with positivity, vitality, and radiant joy.

Chapter: Aquamarines - Gems of Tranquility and Clarity

Aquamarines, with their ethereal blue hues reminiscent of the serene waters of the ocean, hold a timeless allure that speaks to the soul. In this chapter, we embark on a journey to explore the captivating beauty and symbolic significance of aquamarines, and their role as talismans of tranquility and protection.

Origin and Characteristics:

Aquamarines belong to the beryl family of gemstones, sharing their mineral composition with emeralds and morganites. The name "aquamarine" derives from the Latin words "aqua" and "marina," meaning "water of the sea," a fitting tribute to their mesmerizing blue color. Aquamarines range in hue from pale, translucent blues to deeper, more intense shades, with variations in saturation and clarity. Their clarity and transparency allow light to pass through, imparting a luminous glow to the gemstone.
Symbolism and Meaning:

Throughout history, aquamarines have been associated with qualities of serenity, clarity, and harmony. In ancient folklore, aquamarines were believed to be treasured by mermaids and offered as gifts to sailors for protection and safe passage across the seas. Aquamarines are also associated with the throat chakra, encouraging clear communication, self-expression, and inner peace. As symbols of purity and tranquility, aquamarines serve as talismans of serenity and protection, soothing the mind and spirit amidst life's turbulent waters.

Jewelry Applications:

Aquamarines' tranquil blue hues and captivating clarity make them popular choices for jewelry designs. Whether showcased as center stones in rings, pendants, or earrings, or accented with diamonds or other gemstones, aquamarines exude an understated elegance and sophistication. Their versatile color complements a range of metals, from white gold and platinum to yellow gold and rose gold, allowing for endless design possibilities that evoke the calm beauty of the ocean.

Care and Maintenance:

To preserve the beauty and luster of aquamarine jewelry, it is essential to handle and care for it with diligence and caution. Avoid exposing aquamarines to harsh chemicals, extreme temperatures, and abrasive materials, as these may damage the gemstone's surface or setting. Clean aquamarine jewelry regularly with mild soap and warm water, using a soft brush to remove dirt and debris. Store aquamarine jewelry in a soft pouch or lined jewelry box to prevent scratches and protect it from light and humidity.

Spiritual and Healing Properties:

In addition to their aesthetic appeal, aquamarines are believed to possess metaphysical properties that promote emotional balance, clarity, and harmony. Aquamarines are said to calm the mind, soothe the emotions, and enhance spiritual awareness, making them ideal companions for meditation and mindfulness practices. They are also believed to have a purifying effect on the aura and energy field, removing negativity and promoting inner peace and tranquility. Aquamarines, with their soothing blue hues and tranquil energy, offer a sanctuary of serenity and clarity in an often-chaotic world. Whether worn as symbols of protection and guidance or cherished for their inherent beauty and grace, aquamarines continue to inspire and uplift hearts around the globe. So, immerse yourself in the tranquil beauty of aquamarines and let their gentle energy guide you on a journey of inner peace, clarity, and spiritual awakening.

Chapter: Gemstone Projects: Unleashing Radiance in Jewelry Designs

Gemstones, with their captivating colors and inherent beauty, serve as focal points in jewelry designs, adding vibrancy, elegance, and personality to each piece. In this chapter, we explore projects that showcase the exquisite allure of gemstones, from beaded necklaces to gemstone earrings, inviting you to unleash your creativity and create stunning jewelry pieces that celebrate the splendor of natural gemstones.

Beaded Gemstone Necklaces:

Beaded necklaces offer a versatile canvas for showcasing the beauty of gemstones in all their glory. To create a beaded gemstone necklace, start by selecting a variety of gemstone beads in complementary colors, shapes, and sizes. Consider mixing different gemstone types, such as amethysts, citrines, and peridots, to create visual interest and contrast. String the gemstone beads onto beading wire or silk cord, interspersing them with spacer beads or accentuating them with metal findings. Experiment with different bead arrangements and patterns, such as graduated strands, layered necklaces, or multi-strand designs, to achieve the desired look and style.
Gemstone Earrings:

Gemstone earrings offer a dazzling showcase for showcasing the brilliance and beauty of individual gemstones. To create gemstone earrings, start by selecting a pair of gemstone beads or cabochons in your desired shape, color, and size. Choose settings or findings that complement the gemstones and enhance their natural beauty, such as bezel settings, prong settings, or wire-wrapping techniques. Experiment with different earring styles and designs, such as studs, dangles, or chandelier earrings, to suit your personal taste and preferences. Whether you opt for simple solitaire gemstones or intricate multi-stone designs, gemstone earrings add a touch of glamour and sophistication to any ensemble.
Mixed Media Gemstone Bracelets:

Mixed media gemstone bracelets combine the beauty of gemstones with other materials such as metals, crystals, and pearls, creating dynamic and eye-catching jewelry pieces. To create a mixed media gemstone bracelet, start by selecting a variety of gemstone beads in complementary colors and shapes. Incorporate other materials such as metal beads, crystal accents, or freshwater pearls to add texture, dimension, and visual interest to the design. Experiment with different bead weaving techniques, stringing patterns, and wirework elements to create unique and personalized bracelets that reflect your individual style and creativity.

Statement Gemstone Rings:

Statement gemstone rings make bold and striking statements, showcasing the beauty and brilliance of large, faceted gemstones. To create a statement gemstone ring, start by selecting a focal gemstone in a size and shape that commands attention, such as a large amethyst, citrine, or aquamarine. Choose a setting or mounting that complements the gemstone and enhances its natural beauty, such as prong settings, bezel settings, or halo settings. Experiment with different ring designs, band styles, and metal finishes to create a ring that makes a memorable impression and captures the essence of your personal style.

Gemstone projects offer endless opportunities for creativity, exploration, and self-expression, allowing you to unleash your imagination and create jewelry pieces that celebrate the splendor and allure of natural gemstones. Whether you're designing beaded necklaces, gemstone earrings, mixed media bracelets, or statement rings, let the radiant beauty of gemstones inspire your creations and elevate your jewelry-making journey to new heights of elegance and sophistication.

Chapter: Advanced Techniques: Pushing the Boundaries of Jewelry Making

In this chapter, we delve into the world of advanced jewelry making techniques, exploring innovative methods that push the boundaries of traditional craftsmanship and elevate jewelry design to new heights of creativity and sophistication.

Enameling:

Enameling is a centuries-old technique that involves fusing powdered glass onto metal surfaces to create vibrant and durable decorative coatings. To enamel jewelry, start by preparing the metal surface through thorough cleaning and degreasing. Next, apply layers of enamel powder onto the metal using a fine sifter or brush, building up the desired colors and patterns. Fire the piece in a kiln at high temperatures, allowing the enamel to melt and fuse onto the metal surface. Experiment with different enamel colors, techniques such as cloisonné or champlevé, and firing temperatures to achieve stunning and intricate designs.

Etching:

Etching is a process that involves selectively removing metal from a surface using chemicals or acid to create intricate patterns, textures, or designs. To etch jewelry, start by transferring your design onto a metal surface using an etching resist such as vinyl, wax, or photographic emulsion. Apply a solution of ferric chloride or nitric acid to the metal, allowing it to eat away at the exposed areas and create the desired etched design. Rinse the piece thoroughly to remove any remaining etchant and remove the resist to reveal the finished design. Experiment with different resist materials, etching solutions, and techniques such as photo etching or aquatint to create unique and personalized pieces.

Granulation:

Granulation is an ancient technique that involves fusing tiny metal granules onto a metal surface to create intricate patterns, textures, or designs. To granulate jewelry, start by preparing the metal surface through thorough cleaning and degreasing. Next, heat the metal to create a thin layer of oxidation, known as a fire-scale, which acts as a bonding agent for the granules. Sprinkle the metal granules onto the surface and heat the piece again, allowing the granules to fuse onto the metal surface. Experiment with different sizes, shapes, and arrangements of granules to create stunning and intricate designs with a timeless appeal.

Mokume Gane:

Mokume Gane is a Japanese metalworking technique that involves layering and bonding multiple layers of metal to create a distinctive wood-grain pattern. To create Mokume Gane jewelry, start by stacking alternating layers of different metals such as gold, silver, and copper. Heat the metal stack to bond the layers together and then forge or roll the stack to create a thin sheet of metal with a unique pattern. Cut, shape, and form the Mokume Gane metal into jewelry components such as rings, pendants, or earrings, revealing the intricate patterns and colors of the layered metals. Experiment with different metal combinations, layering techniques, and surface finishes to create one-of-a-kind Mokume Gane jewelry pieces that showcase the beauty and complexity of this ancient art form.

Advanced jewelry making techniques offer endless opportunities for creativity, experimentation, and self-expression, allowing artisans to push the boundaries of traditional craftsmanship and create jewelry pieces that are truly works of art. Whether you're exploring the vibrant colors of enamel, the intricate patterns of etching, the delicate textures of granulation, or the mesmerizing patterns of Mokume Gane, advanced techniques invite you to unlock your imagination and elevate your jewelry-making journey to new levels of mastery and innovation.

Chapter: Enameling: Adding Vibrant Colors to Metal

Enameling is a captivating jewelry-making technique that dates back centuries, known for its ability to infuse metal surfaces with vibrant colors and intricate designs. In this chapter, we'll explore the fascinating process of enameling and the endless possibilities it offers for creating stunning and durable decorative coatings on metal jewelry.

Preparation:
Before diving into enameling, it's crucial to prepare your metal surface properly to ensure successful adhesion and fusion of the enamel. Begin by thoroughly cleaning the metal surface with a degreasing solution to remove any dirt, oils, or residues that could interfere with the enameling process. Use a fine abrasive pad or sandpaper to gently roughen the surface, promoting better enamel adhesion. Once cleaned and prepped, ensure the metal is completely dry before proceeding to the next step.

Application:

Enamel powders come in a variety of colors and consistencies, ranging from finely ground powders to coarser grains. Using a fine sifter or brush, apply thin and even layers of enamel powder onto the prepared metal surface. Take care to build up the desired colors and patterns gradually, allowing each layer to dry thoroughly before applying the next. Experiment with different enamel colors, mixing and blending them to create custom hues and effects. For more intricate designs, consider using techniques such as cloisonné, where thin metal wires are fused onto the metal surface to create compartments that hold the enamel, or champlevé, where recessed areas are filled with enamel.

Firing:
Once the enamel has been applied to the metal surface, it's time to fire the piece in a kiln at high temperatures to melt and fuse the enamel onto the metal. The firing process is critical and requires precise temperature control to achieve the desired results without overheating or under-firing the enamel. Follow the manufacturer's instructions for recommended firing temperatures and times based on the type of enamel used. As the piece heats up, watch carefully for the enamel to reach its melting point and begin to flow, creating a smooth and glassy surface. Once fused, allow the piece to cool slowly to prevent thermal shock and ensure the enamel sets properly.

Experimentation:

Enameling offers endless opportunities for experimentation and creativity, allowing artisans to explore a wide range of colors, techniques, and effects. Consider experimenting with different enamel colors, opacities, and textures to create depth and dimension in your designs. Try incorporating other materials such as gold or silver foil, wire, or decorative elements into your enamel work to add contrast and visual interest. Don't be afraid to push the boundaries of traditional enameling techniques and explore innovative approaches to achieve stunning and unique results.

Enameling is a time-honored technique that continues to captivate jewelry makers with its versatility, beauty, and durability. Whether you're a seasoned enamelist or a novice exploring this ancient craft for the first time, enameling offers endless opportunities for artistic expression and creativity. So, gather your enamels, prepare your metal surfaces, and let your imagination soar as you embark on your enameling journey, creating jewelry pieces that shimmer with vibrant colors and timeless beauty.

Chapter: Etching: Unveiling the Beauty of Intricate Designs

Etching is a fascinating and versatile technique in jewelry making, offering artisans the ability to create intricate patterns, textures, and designs on metal surfaces. In this chapter, we'll explore the process of etching and the various methods and materials used to achieve stunning and personalized results.

Design Preparation:

Before beginning the etching process, it's essential to prepare your design and transfer it onto the metal surface. Start by creating or selecting a design that reflects your artistic vision, whether it's a geometric pattern, botanical motif, or abstract composition. Transfer the design onto the metal surface using an etching resist, such as vinyl, wax, or photographic emulsion. Secure the resist firmly to the metal to prevent any leakage or seepage of the etching solution.

Etching Solution:
The etching solution is a key component of the etching process, as it selectively removes metal from the exposed areas of the metal surface. Common etching solutions include ferric chloride or nitric acid, each offering different etching properties and effects. Prepare the etching solution according to the manufacturer's instructions, taking care to handle it safely and wear protective gear such as gloves and goggles to prevent skin contact and eye irritation.

Etching Process:
Once the design is securely transferred onto the metal surface and the etching solution is prepared, it's time to begin the etching process. Submerge the metal piece in the etching solution, ensuring that the exposed areas of the design are fully submerged and in contact with the solution. Monitor the etching process closely, periodically agitating the solution to promote even etching and prevent uneven results. The etching time will vary depending on factors such as the type of metal, the depth of the etch, and the strength of the etching solution. Once the desired depth of etching is achieved, remove the metal piece from the etching solution and rinse it thoroughly with water to neutralize the acid and stop the etching process.

Finishing Touches:

After the etching process is complete, remove the etching resist from the metal surface to reveal the finished design. Use a gentle abrasive pad or fine sandpaper to remove any remaining resist residue and clean the metal surface. If desired, further enhance the design by adding additional surface treatments such as patinas, enamels, or polishing to highlight the etched areas and create contrast and depth.

Experimentation and Exploration:
Etching offers endless opportunities for experimentation and exploration, allowing artisans to push the boundaries of traditional techniques and create unique and personalized pieces. Experiment with different resist materials, etching solutions, and techniques such as photo etching or aquatint to achieve a wide range of effects and styles. Don't be afraid to explore unconventional materials or combine etching with other jewelry-making techniques to create truly one-of-a-kind pieces that reflect your artistic vision and creativity.

Etching is a versatile and rewarding technique that empowers jewelry makers to unleash their creativity and express their unique style through intricate and personalized designs. Whether you're drawn to the precision of photo etching, the organic textures of aquatint, or the boldness of traditional etching, etching offers endless possibilities for creating jewelry pieces that captivate and inspire. So, gather your materials, prepare your designs, and let your imagination soar as you embark on your etching journey, creating jewelry pieces that leave a lasting impression.

Chapter: Granulation: Crafting Timeless Beauty with Tiny Granules

Granulation is an ancient jewelry-making technique that has captivated artisans for centuries with its ability to create intricate patterns and textures using tiny metal granules. In this chapter, we'll delve into the art of granulation and explore the steps involved in creating exquisite jewelry pieces adorned with delicate granular motifs.

Surface Preparation:

Before embarking on the granulation process, it's essential to prepare the metal surface to ensure optimal adhesion and fusion of the granules. Start by thoroughly cleaning and degreasing the metal surface to remove any dirt, oils, or residues that could interfere with the granulation process. Next, heat the metal to create a thin layer of oxidation, known as a fire-scale, which serves as a bonding agent for the granules. This oxidation layer provides a textured surface for the granules to adhere to and enhances the overall aesthetic of the finished piece.

Granule Application:
Once the metal surface is prepared, it's time to apply the metal granules. Metal granules are typically made from the same metal as the base metal, such as gold, silver, or copper, and come in a variety of sizes, shapes, and textures. Using a fine brush or tweezers, carefully sprinkle the granules onto the prepared metal surface, arranging them according to your desired design or pattern. Take care to space the granules evenly and avoid overcrowding, as this can affect the overall appearance and integrity of the design.

Fusing Process:
With the granules in place, it's time to fuse them onto the metal surface. Heat the metal piece gradually, using a torch or kiln to reach the appropriate temperature for the metal to melt and the granules to fuse. As the metal granules begin to heat up, they will soften and merge with the underlying metal surface, creating a strong and durable bond. It's essential to monitor the heating process closely to prevent overheating or melting of the granules, which can result in distortion or loss of detail in the design. Once the granules are fully fused, allow the piece to cool slowly to prevent thermal shock and ensure the integrity of the granulated design.

Finishing Touches:

After the granulation process is complete, the piece may require additional finishing touches to enhance its appearance and durability. Use abrasive pads or polishing compounds to remove any excess oxidation or fire-scale from the surface and reveal the luster and shine of the metal. If desired, further enhance the granulated design by adding additional textures, patinas, or surface treatments to create depth and contrast.

Experimentation and Exploration:
Granulation offers endless opportunities for experimentation and exploration, allowing artisans to create intricate and personalized designs that showcase their unique style and creativity. Experiment with different sizes, shapes, and arrangements of granules to create a wide range of effects and motifs, from delicate floral patterns to geometric designs. Combine granulation with other jewelry-making techniques such as soldering, engraving, or stone-setting to create truly one-of-a-kind pieces that reflect your artistic vision and passion.

Granulation is a time-honored technique that continues to inspire and enchant jewelry makers with its timeless beauty and intricate detail. Whether you're a seasoned granulation artist or a novice exploring this ancient craft for the first time, granulation offers endless possibilities for creating jewelry pieces that captivate the imagination and evoke a sense of wonder. So, gather your granules, prepare your metal surfaces, and let your creativity soar as you embark on your granulation journey, creating jewelry pieces that stand the test of time and leave a lasting legacy of craftsmanship and artistry.

Chapter: Mokume Gane: Unveiling the Beauty of Layered Metals

Mokume Gane, translated as "wood grain metal" in Japanese, is a captivating metalworking technique that originated in feudal Japan. This ancient art form involves layering and bonding multiple sheets of different metals to create a unique and mesmerizing wood-grain pattern. In this chapter, we'll explore the intricate process of creating Mokume Gane jewelry and the breathtaking results it yields.

Selection of Metals:

The essence of Mokume Gane lies in the harmonious interplay of different metals, each contributing its unique color, texture, and properties to the final piece. Traditionally, Mokume Gane utilizes combinations of precious metals such as gold, silver, and copper. However, contemporary artisans often experiment with a wide range of metals, including platinum, palladium, and titanium, to achieve diverse and striking effects.

Layering and Bonding:
To begin the Mokume Gane process, artisans meticulously stack alternating layers of metal sheets, carefully considering the desired pattern and color composition. The metal stack is then tightly bound or clamped together to ensure even pressure and contact between the layers. Through the application of heat and pressure, the metals are bonded together, forming a solid billet with distinct layers.

Forging and Pattern Development:
Once the metal stack is bonded, it undergoes a series of forging and annealing cycles to refine and elongate the billet. During forging, the metal layers are compressed and stretched, causing them to flow and intermix, resulting in the characteristic wood-grain pattern. Artisans employ various forging techniques, such as twisting, folding, and rolling, to manipulate the metal layers and enhance the intricacy of the pattern.

Material Reduction and Sheet Formation:

After forging, the Mokume Gane billet is progressively reduced in thickness through rolling or hammering, gradually revealing the intricate patterns and colors of the layered metals. The metal sheet is annealed periodically to relieve stress and prevent cracking during the reduction process. As the billet is further refined, artisans meticulously monitor the development of the wood-grain pattern, adjusting the pressure and direction of the rolling or hammering to achieve the desired aesthetic.

Jewelry Component Fabrication:
Once the Mokume Gane sheet reaches the desired thickness and pattern, it is ready to be transformed into jewelry components such as rings, pendants, or earrings. Artisans carefully cut, shape, and form the metal sheet using traditional metalworking techniques, preserving the integrity of the pattern, and showcasing its beauty. Each jewelry piece is meticulously finished, ensuring a seamless blend of craftsmanship and artistry.

Surface Finishing and Enhancement:
To enhance the beauty and durability of Mokume Gane jewelry, artisans may apply surface treatments such as polishing, patination, or etching. These finishing techniques serve to highlight the contrast and depth of the wood-grain pattern, imbuing the jewelry with a sense of refinement and elegance.

Mokume Gane is a testament to the mastery of metalworking and the enduring allure of handmade craftsmanship. With its rich history, intricate patterns, and mesmerizing beauty, Mokume Gane continues to captivate and inspire artisans and jewelry enthusiasts around the world. Whether as a symbol of tradition, a celebration of nature, or an expression of artistic expression, Mokume Gane jewelry invites us to embrace the beauty of layered metals and the timeless artistry of the human hand.

Chapter: Mastering Advanced Jewelry Making Techniques

Embarking on the journey of mastering advanced jewelry making techniques requires dedication, patience, and a willingness to experiment. In this chapter, we'll delve into step-by-step instructions for honing your skills in enameling, etching, granulation, and Mokume Gane, guiding you through each technique to unlock your creativity and craftsmanship.

Enameling:
Step 1: Prepare the Metal Surface

Clean the metal surface thoroughly to remove any dirt, grease, or oxidation.
Degrease the metal using a mild detergent or solvent to ensure proper adhesion of the enamel.
Step 2: Apply the Enamel

Select the desired enamel colors and prepare them by grinding them into a fine powder.
Using a sifter or brush, apply a thin layer of enamel powder onto the metal surface, ensuring even coverage.
Experiment with different application techniques, such as wet packing or dry dusting, to achieve various effects.
Step 3: Firing the Enamel

Place the enameled piece onto a kiln shelf or firing trivet and carefully transfer it into the kiln.
Fire the piece in the kiln at the recommended temperature and duration for the type of enamel used.
Monitor the firing process to ensure the enamel fuses evenly onto the metal surface without over-firing or under-firing.
Step 4: Finishing Touches

Allow the enameled piece to cool slowly inside the kiln to prevent thermal shock and cracking.

Once cooled, inspect the enamel surface for any imperfections or unevenness.
If necessary, perform additional firings or touch-ups to achieve the desired finish and appearance.

Etching:

Step 1: Prepare the Metal Surface

Choose a suitable metal for etching, such as copper, brass, or silver, and cut it to the desired size and shape.
Clean the metal surface thoroughly to remove any oils, dirt, or debris that may interfere with the etching process.

Step 2: Apply the Etching Resist

Transfer your design or pattern onto the metal surface using an etching resist such as vinyl, wax, or photographic emulsion.
Ensure that the resist is firmly adhered to the metal and covers the areas you wish to protect from etching.

Step 3: Etching Process

Prepare the etching solution according to the manufacturer's instructions, ensuring proper safety precautions are observed.
Submerge the metal into the etching solution, allowing the acid to eat away at the exposed areas and create the desired etched design.
Monitor the etching process closely, periodically checking the metal's progress to avoid over-etching.

Step 4: Final Steps

Once the etching is complete, remove the metal from the etching solution and rinse it thoroughly with water to neutralize the acid.
Remove the etching resist to reveal the finished design, taking care not to damage the metal surface.

Clean the etched metal with a mild detergent or solvent to remove any residue and prepare it for further finishing or assembly.

Granulation:

Step 1: Prepare the Metal Surface

Clean the metal surface thoroughly to remove any dirt, grease, or oxidation.
Heat the metal to create a thin layer of oxidation, known as a fire-scale, which acts as a bonding agent for the granules.

Step 2: Apply the Metal Granules

Select metal granules of the desired size, shape, and composition for your granulation project.
Sprinkle the metal granules onto the metal surface, ensuring even distribution and coverage of the desired areas.

Step 3: Fusing the Granules

Heat the metal surface to a temperature that allows the granules to fuse onto the metal without melting or deforming.
Use a torch or kiln to carefully heat the metal, ensuring uniform heating and adequate bonding of the granules.

Step 4: Finishing Touches

Allow the granulated metal to cool slowly to prevent thermal shock and ensure proper bonding.
Inspect the granulation for any gaps or irregularities and perform any necessary touch-ups or repairs.
Clean the granulated metal surface with a mild detergent or solvent to remove any residual flux or oxidation.

Mokume Gane:

Step 1: Prepare the Metal Layers

Select a combination of metals for your Mokume Gane project, such as gold, silver, and copper.

Cut the metal sheets into uniform sizes and stack them in alternating layers, ensuring a tight and secure fit.

Step 2: Bonding the Metal Layers

Apply pressure to the metal stack using a hydraulic press, rolling mill, or hammer to bond the layers together.
Heat the metal stack to a temperature that allows the metals to fuse without melting or deforming.

Step 3: Forging and Pattern Development

Forge or roll the bonded metal stack to elongate and refine the pattern, creating the characteristic wood-grain effect.
Experiment with different forging techniques and pressure levels to manipulate the metal layers and enhance the pattern's intricacy.

Step 4: Sheet Formation and Fabrication

Reduce the thickness of the Mokume Gane billet through rolling or hammering, gradually revealing the pattern and colors of the layered metals.
Cut, shape, and form the Mokume Gane sheet into jewelry components such as rings, pendants, or earrings, preserving the integrity of the pattern.

Step 5: Surface Finishing and Enhancement

Apply surface treatments such as polishing, patination, or etching to enhance the beauty and contrast of the Mokume Gane pattern.
Ensure a seamless blend of craftsmanship and artistry in the finished jewelry piece, showcasing the unique and mesmerizing beauty of Mokume Gane.

Conclusion:

Mastering advanced jewelry making techniques requires practice, experimentation, and a willingness to learn from both successes and failures. By following these step-by-step instructions and immersing yourself in the intricacies of enameling, etching, granulation, and Mokume Gane, you'll unlock new realms of creativity and craftsmanship in your jewelry-making journey. So, gather your tools, materials, and inspiration, and embark on the path to mastery, where each technique becomes a brushstroke in the canvas of your artistic expression.

Chapter: Projects Showcasing the Versatility of Advanced Techniques

In this chapter, we'll explore a variety of jewelry-making projects that showcase the versatility and beauty of advanced techniques such as enameling, etching, granulation, and Mokume Gane. From colorful enameled pendants to intricately etched earrings and elegantly granulated rings, these projects will inspire you to experiment with these techniques and unleash your creativity.

Enamel Pendant with Cloisonné Design:
Create a stunning enamel pendant featuring a intricate cloisonné design, showcasing the vibrant colors and intricate patterns of this ancient technique.

Materials:

Copper or silver sheet
Enamel powders in various colors
Cloisonné wires
Sifter or brush
Kiln
Jewelry findings (bail, chain)
Instructions:

Cut the metal sheet into a pendant shape and clean the surface thoroughly.

Bend the cloisonné wires into desired shapes and solder them onto the metal surface to create the cloisonné design.

Apply layers of enamel powder within the cloisonné cells, alternating colors as desired.

Fire the pendant in the kiln at the appropriate temperature to melt and fuse the enamel.

Allow the pendant to cool, then polish and finish the surface to reveal the vibrant cloisonné design.

Attach a bail to the pendant and string it onto a chain to complete the necklace.

Etched Earrings with Botanical Motifs:

Design a pair of elegant earrings featuring intricate botanical motifs etched onto metal, highlighting the delicate beauty of nature.

Materials:

Copper or brass sheet
Etching resist (vinyl, wax, or emulsion)
Etching solution (ferric chloride or nitric acid)
Scribe or marker
Jewelry findings (earring hooks, jump rings)
Instructions:

Cut the metal sheet into earring shapes and clean the surface thoroughly.

Transfer your botanical designs onto the metal surface using an etching resist.

Etch the metal in the appropriate etching solution, following safety precautions.

Remove the resist and clean the metal to reveal the etched designs.

Add earring hooks and jump rings to the etched metal pieces to create earrings.

Polish and finish the earrings to enhance the beauty of the etched motifs.

Granulated Ring with Geometric Patterns:

Craft a unique granulated ring featuring geometric patterns created with tiny metal granules, showcasing the intricate artistry of granulation.

Materials:

Silver or gold sheet
Metal granules
Flux
Torch
Jewelry mandrel
Jewelry hammer
Instructions:

Cut the metal sheet into a ring band and clean the surface thoroughly.

Apply flux to the metal surface and heat it with a torch to create a fire-scale.

Sprinkle metal granules onto the flux-coated surface to create geometric patterns.

Heat the metal again to fuse the granules onto the surface, using a torch or kiln.

Shape the ring band around a mandrel to form the desired ring size and shape.

Polish and finish the ring to highlight the intricate granulation patterns.

Mokume Gane Cuff Bracelet:

Craft a stunning cuff bracelet featuring a mesmerizing Mokume Gane pattern, showcasing the unique beauty of layered metals.

Materials:

Mokume Gane billet (prepared or handmade)
Rolling mill or hydraulic press
Jewelry saw
Jewelry files
Jewelry mandrel
Instructions:

Obtain or create a Mokume Gane billet using layers of different metals.
Forge or roll the billet to elongate and refine the pattern.
Cut the billet into a cuff bracelet shape using a jewelry saw.
Shape the cuff bracelet around a mandrel to achieve the desired size and curvature.
File and finish the edges of the bracelet to ensure a smooth and comfortable fit.
Polish and buff the bracelet to enhance the luster and contrast of the Mokume Gane pattern.

Conclusion:

These projects demonstrate the versatility and beauty of advanced jewelry-making techniques, from the vibrant colors of enameling to the intricate patterns of etching, granulation, and Mokume Gane. Whether you're drawn to the rich hues of enamel, the delicate details of etching, or the mesmerizing patterns of Mokume Gane, these projects offer endless opportunities for creativity and self-expression. So, gather your tools and materials, and embark on a journey of exploration and discovery as you create stunning jewelry pieces that showcase the magic of advanced techniques.

Chapter: Design and Inspiration

Finding inspiration is essential for creating unique and captivating jewelry designs. In this chapter, we'll explore various tips and techniques for seeking inspiration and translating it into stunning jewelry pieces that reflect your style, passion, and creativity.

Nature's Beauty:
Nature is a boundless source of inspiration for jewelry designers. Take a walk in the park, hike through the mountains, or stroll along the beach to immerse yourself in the beauty of the natural world. Observe the intricate patterns of leaves, the delicate structure of flowers, or the mesmerizing colors of gemstones found in nature. Let the shapes, textures, and colors you encounter inspire your jewelry designs, whether it's a leaf-shaped pendant, a flower-inspired ring, or a gemstone necklace reflecting the hues of the sea.

Cultural Heritage:
Explore the rich tapestry of world cultures and traditions for inspiration in jewelry design. Study ancient civilizations, indigenous tribes, and cultural artifacts to uncover motifs, symbols, and techniques that resonate with you. Incorporate elements of folklore, mythology, and symbolism into your designs, paying homage to the traditions and stories of different cultures. Whether it's the intricate filigree of Eastern jewelry, the bold geometric patterns of African adornments, or the ornate motifs of Celtic art, draw inspiration from diverse cultures to create jewelry pieces that celebrate heritage and diversity.

Art and Architecture:

Expand your horizons by exploring the realms of art and architecture for inspiration. Visit museums, galleries, and architectural landmarks to admire the work of renowned artists and architects. Study the lines, shapes, and proportions of sculptures, paintings, and buildings to glean insights into composition, form, and structure. Let the fluid curves of Art Nouveau, the geometric precision of Art Deco, or the minimalist elegance of Bauhaus inspire your jewelry designs. Experiment with abstract motifs, architectural elements, and artistic techniques to create jewelry pieces that blur the boundaries between art and adornment.

Personal Stories and Emotions:
Tap into your own experiences, memories, and emotions for inspiration in jewelry design. Reflect on significant moments, milestones, and relationships in your life, and translate them into wearable symbols and talismans. Whether it's a birthstone necklace commemorating a special birthday, a charm bracelet representing cherished memories, or a custom-designed engagement ring symbolizing everlasting love, infuse your jewelry designs with personal meaning and sentiment. Draw inspiration from your own journey and storytelling to create jewelry pieces that resonate with authenticity and depth.

Experimentation and Innovation:

Embrace experimentation and innovation as catalysts for inspiration in jewelry design. Push the boundaries of traditional techniques, materials, and aesthetics to explore new possibilities and challenge conventions. Play with unexpected combinations, unconventional materials, and avant-garde concepts to push the boundaries of your creativity. Whether it's incorporating unconventional materials like resin, found objects, or recycled materials into your designs, or experimenting with cutting-edge technologies like 3D printing or laser cutting, let curiosity and imagination guide your exploration of new frontiers in jewelry design.

Conclusion:

Finding inspiration is a deeply personal and enriching journey that fuels creativity and innovation in jewelry design. Whether you seek inspiration in nature's beauty, cultural heritage, art and architecture, personal stories, or experimentation, the key is to remain open-minded, curious, and receptive to the world around you. Keep a sketchbook handy to capture ideas, images, and musings that spark your imagination, and allow yourself the freedom to explore and experiment without fear of failure. By embracing inspiration as a continuous and evolving process, you'll uncover endless possibilities for creating jewelry pieces that are as unique and authentic as you are.

Chapter: Guidance on Developing a Personal Style

Developing a personal style is essential for jewelry designers to create cohesive, distinctive, and meaningful pieces that resonate with their audience. In this chapter, we'll explore practical guidance and strategies for discovering, refining, and expressing your unique aesthetic in jewelry design.

Self-Reflection and Exploration:
Start by embarking on a journey of self-reflection and exploration to uncover your personal tastes, preferences, and values. Reflect on your personality, lifestyle, and cultural influences to identify themes, motifs, and elements that resonate with you. Consider your favorite colors, textures, and materials, as well as your aesthetic preferences, whether it's minimalist and modern, bohemian and eclectic, or vintage and romantic. Experiment with different styles, techniques, and materials to discover what feels most authentic and true to your vision.

Identify Inspirations and Influences:
Draw inspiration from a diverse array of sources, including art, fashion, nature, culture, and personal experiences. Explore your interests, passions, and curiosities to uncover themes, motifs, and symbols that inspire and resonate with you. Study the work of renowned jewelry designers, artists, and artisans to gain insights into their creative processes, techniques, and aesthetics. Identify key elements, such as colors, shapes, textures, and materials, that appeal to you and incorporate them into your own designs in unique and innovative ways.

Cultivate Consistency and Cohesion:
Strive to cultivate consistency and cohesion in your jewelry designs to establish a recognizable and cohesive brand identity. Define your signature style by refining your aesthetic preferences, design principles, and visual language. Consider factors such as materials, techniques, colors, and forms that consistently appear across your designs, creating a cohesive and harmonious body of work. Aim for clarity, coherence, and authenticity in your design choices to convey a strong and cohesive brand identity that resonates with your target audience.

Embrace Experimentation and Evolution:
Embrace experimentation and evolution as essential components of your creative journey in jewelry design. Allow yourself the freedom to explore new techniques, materials, and aesthetics, and to push the boundaries of your comfort zone. Experiment with unexpected combinations, unconventional materials, and avant-garde concepts to challenge conventions and spark innovation. Remain open-minded, curious, and receptive to new ideas, feedback, and experiences, and embrace the process of continuous learning and growth as a jewelry designer.

Tell Your Story:

Infuse your jewelry designs with personal meaning, stories, and symbolism to create connections and resonate with your audience on a deeper level. Draw inspiration from your own experiences, memories, and emotions to imbue your designs with authenticity, depth, and resonance. Whether it's incorporating symbols, motifs, or materials that hold personal significance, or infusing your designs with narratives and storytelling, let your jewelry pieces reflect your unique journey, values, and perspective. By sharing your story through your designs, you'll create meaningful connections with your audience and establish a lasting and authentic brand identity.

Conclusion:

Developing a personal style is a dynamic and ongoing process that requires self-awareness, exploration, and experimentation. By reflecting on your personal tastes, identifying inspirations and influences, cultivating consistency and cohesion, embracing experimentation and evolution, and telling your story through your designs, you'll create jewelry pieces that are as unique and authentic as you are. Stay true to yourself, trust your instincts, and let your creativity soar as you embark on your journey to develop and express your personal style in jewelry design.

Chapter: Exercises and Prompts to Spark Creativity

Creativity is the lifeblood of jewelry design, fueling innovation, exploration, and expression. In this chapter, we'll explore a variety of exercises and prompts designed to ignite your imagination, inspire fresh ideas, and unleash your creativity in jewelry making.

Nature Walk Inspiration:
Take a nature walk and immerse yourself in the sights, sounds, and textures of the natural world. Observe the intricate patterns of leaves, the vibrant colors of flowers, and the textures of bark and stones. Collect found objects such as leaves, twigs, and feathers, and use them as inspiration for designing jewelry pieces. Experiment with incorporating organic shapes, textures, and colors into your designs, drawing inspiration from the beauty and diversity of nature.

Mood Board Exploration:

Create a mood board by collecting images, textures, colors, and materials that resonate with you and evoke a particular mood or theme. Use magazines, catalogs, and online sources to gather inspiration and create a visual collage that reflects your aesthetic preferences and design aspirations. Explore themes such as vintage romance, modern minimalism, bohemian chic, or geometric abstraction, and use your mood board as a springboard for generating ideas and concepts for jewelry designs.

Storytelling Through Symbols:
Select a theme, narrative, or personal story that resonates with you and explore ways to translate it into jewelry designs. Identify symbols, motifs, and imagery that represent key elements of the story and incorporate them into your designs with intention and meaning. Whether it's a symbol of love, strength, or transformation, infuse your jewelry pieces with symbolism and storytelling to create connections and resonate with your audience on a deeper level.

Material Exploration:
Experiment with different materials, textures, and techniques to push the boundaries of traditional jewelry making and spark creativity. Explore unconventional materials such as found objects, recycled materials, or natural elements like wood, feathers, or shells, and integrate them into your designs in unexpected ways. Combine contrasting materials such as metal and fabric, glass and stone, or leather and beads to create dynamic and visually intriguing jewelry pieces that defy conventions and inspire curiosity.

Collaboration and Community:

Engage with other jewelry makers, artists, and creatives in your community or online forums to exchange ideas, share inspiration, and collaborate on projects. Participate in collaborative challenges, workshops, or design competitions to stretch your creative muscles and gain fresh perspectives. Embrace feedback, constructive criticism, and support from fellow makers to refine your ideas, overcome creative blocks, and elevate your craftsmanship to new heights.

Conclusion:

Creativity is a journey of exploration, experimentation, and expression, fueled by curiosity, inspiration, and collaboration. By engaging in exercises and prompts that spark creativity, you'll unlock new insights, ideas, and possibilities in your jewelry making practice. Whether it's drawing inspiration from nature, exploring themes through mood boards, storytelling through symbols, experimenting with materials, or collaborating with others, embrace the process of creativity as a joyful and enriching pursuit that fuels your passion and drives your artistic vision in jewelry design.

Chapter: Finishing Touches

Finishing touches are the final steps in the jewelry making process that elevate your pieces from raw materials to polished works of art. In this chapter, we'll explore different finishing techniques that add luster, depth, and character to your jewelry designs, enhancing their beauty and appeal.

Polishing:
Polishing is a technique used to create a smooth, shiny surface on metal jewelry components, removing scratches, imperfections, and oxidation. To polish jewelry, use polishing compounds and abrasives such as polishing cloths, buffing wheels, or rotary tools equipped with polishing attachments. Apply the polishing compound to the metal surface and buff in a circular motion until the desired shine is achieved. Experiment with different polishing compounds and techniques to achieve various levels of shine and luster, from satin finishes to mirror-like reflections.

Patina:

Patina is a surface treatment that adds color, texture, and depth to metal jewelry, creating an aged or antique appearance. To apply a patina to your jewelry, use chemical solutions such as liver of sulfur or blackening agents to darken the metal surface. Apply the patina solution using a brush or dipping method and allow it to react with the metal to achieve the desired color and effect. Use techniques such as brushing, buffing, or antiquing to highlight raised areas and create contrast in the patina. Experiment with different patina solutions, application methods, and sealing techniques to create unique and distinctive finishes that complement your jewelry designs.

Oxidation:
Oxidation is a natural process that occurs when metal reacts with oxygen in the air, forming a thin layer of oxide on the surface of the metal. Oxidation can be controlled and manipulated to create decorative effects on jewelry, such as darkening silver or enhancing texture and detail. To oxidize jewelry, use chemical solutions or fumes such as liver of sulfur or ammonia to darken the metal surface. Apply the oxidation solution selectively to areas of the jewelry where you want to create contrast or enhance detail and allow it to react with the metal for the desired amount of time. Rinse the jewelry thoroughly to remove excess oxidation solution and neutralize the metal surface, and buff with a polishing cloth to reveal the finished effect.

Finishing Seals:

Once your jewelry has been polished, patinated, or oxidized, apply a finishing sealant or lacquer to protect the surface and preserve the finish. Finishing sealants come in various forms, including spray-on coatings, brush-on lacquers, or wax-based finishes. Apply the sealant evenly to the metal surface using a brush or applicator and allow it to dry completely before handling or wearing the jewelry. Finishing sealants provide a protective barrier against tarnish, oxidation, and wear, prolonging the life of your jewelry and maintaining its beauty and luster over time.

Conclusion:

Finishing touches are the final steps in the jewelry making process that add depth, character, and beauty to your creations. Whether it's polishing to achieve a smooth, shiny surface, applying a patina for an aged or antique appearance, oxidizing to enhance texture and detail, or sealing to protect the finish, each finishing technique adds a unique and distinctive element to your jewelry designs. Experiment with different finishing techniques, materials, and application methods to discover the perfect combination that brings your jewelry to life and captivates the senses of those who wear and admire your creations.

Chapter: Polishing

Polishing is a crucial step in the jewelry making process that transforms raw metal into gleaming, refined pieces. Whether you're working with silver, gold, brass, or other metals, mastering the art of polishing can enhance the beauty and allure of your jewelry creations. In this chapter, we'll explore the techniques and tools involved in achieving a flawless polish on your metal jewelry components.

Preparation:
Before you begin polishing, ensure that your jewelry components are clean and free from any dirt, grease, or debris. Use a mild detergent or jewelry cleaner to remove any surface contaminants, and dry the pieces thoroughly with a soft, lint-free cloth. Inspect the metal surface for scratches, blemishes, or oxidation that may need to be addressed during the polishing process.

Selecting Polishing Compounds:

Choose the appropriate polishing compound for the metal you're working with and the level of shine you wish to achieve. Polishing compounds come in various forms, including pastes, creams, and bars, each formulated for specific metals and finishes. For example, tripoli or brown rouge compounds are commonly used for initial polishing on metals like brass and copper, while jeweler's rouge or rouge compounds are ideal for achieving a high shine on precious metals like silver and gold.

Using Polishing Tools:
Depending on the size and shape of your jewelry components, you can use a variety of polishing tools to achieve the desired finish. For small or intricate pieces, polishing cloths or buffing pads mounted on a rotary tool can provide precise control and access to hard-to-reach areas. Alternatively, larger pieces may benefit from buffing wheels mounted on a bench grinder or polishing motor, allowing for faster and more efficient polishing over larger surface areas.

Polishing Technique:
Apply a small amount of polishing compound to the metal surface, focusing on one section at a time. Using gentle pressure, buff the compound into the metal using a circular or back-and-forth motion, ensuring even coverage and consistent results. As you polish, periodically inspect the metal surface to assess the progress and adjust your technique as needed to achieve the desired level of shine and luster.

Finishing Touches:

Once you've completed the initial polishing, use a clean, dry cloth to remove any excess polishing compound and inspect the metal surface for any remaining imperfections. If necessary, repeat the polishing process with a finer polishing compound to further refine the finish and remove any remaining scratches or blemishes. Finally, buff the metal surface to a brilliant shine using a clean polishing cloth or buffing wheel, taking care to avoid over-polishing, and causing damage to the metal.

Conclusion:

Polishing is an essential skill in jewelry making that can elevate your creations from ordinary to extraordinary. By mastering the techniques and tools of polishing, you can achieve a flawless finish that highlights the beauty and craftsmanship of your metal jewelry components. Experiment with different polishing compounds, tools, and techniques to discover the perfect combination that brings your jewelry designs to life and captivates the senses of those who wear and admire your creations.

Chapter: Patina

Patina is a transformative surface treatment that imbues metal jewelry with character, depth, and a sense of history. By adding color, texture, and dimension, patina can elevate your jewelry creations, giving them an antique, weathered, or rustic appearance. In this chapter, we'll explore the techniques and methods for applying patina to metal jewelry components, allowing you to unleash your creativity and infuse your designs with a unique and distinctive allure.

Preparation:
Before applying patina, ensure that your metal jewelry components are clean and free from any dirt, grease, or residues. Use a mild detergent or jewelry cleaner to remove any surface contaminants, and dry the pieces thoroughly with a soft, lint-free cloth. Patina adheres best to metals with a matte or lightly textured surface, so consider sanding or etching the metal to create a suitable substrate for the patina.

Choosing Patina Solutions:

Select the appropriate patina solution for the metal you're working with and the desired effect you wish to achieve. Common patina solutions include liver of sulfur, ferric nitrate, and blackening agents, each offering unique colors and effects when applied to different metals. Experiment with diluting the patina solution with water or varying the application time to control the intensity and depth of the patina.

Applying Patina:
There are several methods for applying patina to metal jewelry, including brushing, dipping, spraying, and sponging. Brushing involves applying the patina solution directly onto the metal surface using a brush or sponge, allowing you to control the application and create subtle variations in color and texture. Dipping involves immersing the metal components into the patina solution for a predetermined amount of time, resulting in a uniform and consistent patina across the entire surface.

Enhancing the Patina:
Once the patina solution has been applied, experiment with techniques such as brushing, buffing, or antiquing to enhance the texture and contrast of the patina. Use fine steel wool or abrasive pads to gently remove some of the patina from raised areas, revealing the underlying metal, and creating highlights and dimension. Alternatively, apply additional layers of patina solution or use a torch to selectively darken or oxidize specific areas of the metal, adding depth and complexity to the patina.

Sealing the Patina:

To protect the patina and prevent it from fading or tarnishing over time, consider sealing the metal surface with a clear lacquer or sealant. Apply the sealant evenly over the entire surface of the patina using a brush or spray applicator and allow it to dry completely before handling or wearing the jewelry. Be sure to follow the manufacturer's instructions for proper application and curing of the sealant to ensure maximum durability and longevity of the patina.

Conclusion:

Patina offers jewelry makers a versatile and creative way to add character and personality to their metal creations. By experimenting with different patina solutions, application methods, and finishing techniques, you can achieve a wide range of effects and create jewelry pieces that tell a story and evoke emotion. Embrace the art of patina, and let your imagination soar as you explore the endless possibilities of this ancient surface treatment, transforming ordinary metal into extraordinary works of art.

Chapter: Oxidation

Oxidation is a fascinating process that occurs naturally when metals interact with oxygen in the air, resulting in the formation of a thin layer of oxide on the metal surface. While oxidation can sometimes be viewed as undesirable, it can also be harnessed and manipulated to create unique and decorative effects in jewelry making. In this chapter, we'll explore the techniques and methods for oxidizing metal jewelry components, allowing you to infuse your designs with depth, contrast, and character.

Preparation:
Before oxidizing your jewelry components, ensure that they are clean and free from any dirt, oils, or residues. Use a mild detergent or jewelry cleaner to remove any surface contaminants, and dry the pieces thoroughly with a soft, lint-free cloth. Oxidation solutions adhere best to metals with a matte or lightly textured surface, so consider sanding or etching the metal to create a suitable substrate for the oxidation.

Choosing Oxidation Solutions:

Select the appropriate oxidation solution for the metal you're working with and the desired effect you wish to achieve. Common oxidation solutions include liver of sulfur, ammonia, and proprietary patina solutions, each offering unique colors and effects when applied to different metals. Experiment with diluting the oxidation solution with water or varying the application time to control the intensity and depth of the oxidation.

Applying Oxidation:
There are several methods for applying oxidation to metal jewelry, including brushing, dipping, spraying, and fuming. Brushing involves applying the oxidation solution directly onto the metal surface using a brush or sponge, allowing you to control the application and create subtle variations in color and texture. Dipping involves immersing the metal components into the oxidation solution for a predetermined amount of time, resulting in a uniform and consistent oxidation across the entire surface.

Enhancing the Oxidation:
Once the oxidation solution has been applied, experiment with techniques such as brushing, buffing, or antiquing to enhance the texture and contrast of the oxidation. Use fine steel wool or abrasive pads to gently remove some of the oxidation from raised areas, revealing the underlying metal, and creating highlights and dimension. Alternatively, apply additional layers of oxidation solution or use a torch to selectively darken or oxidize specific areas of the metal, adding depth and complexity to the overall effect.

Sealing the Oxidation (optional):

While oxidation can enhance the appearance of metal jewelry, it may also be prone to fading or tarnishing over time if not properly sealed. Consider sealing the oxidized metal surface with a clear lacquer or sealant to protect it from environmental factors and preserve the oxidation effect. Apply the sealant evenly over the entire surface of the oxidized metal using a brush or spray applicator and allow it to dry completely before handling or wearing the jewelry.

Conclusion:

Oxidation offers jewelry makers a versatile and creative way to add depth, contrast, and character to their metal creations. By experimenting with different oxidation solutions, application methods, and finishing techniques, you can achieve a wide range of effects and create jewelry pieces that exude a sense of timelessness and intrigue. Embrace the art of oxidation, and let your imagination soar as you explore the endless possibilities of this ancient surface treatment, transforming ordinary metal into extraordinary works of art.

Chapter: Finishing Seals

After investing time and effort into creating beautiful jewelry pieces, it's essential to protect the surface and preserve the finish to ensure their longevity and beauty. Finishing seals provide a protective barrier against tarnish, oxidation, and wear, helping to maintain the integrity and appearance of your jewelry over time. In this chapter, we'll explore the different types of finishing seals available and provide guidelines for their application.

Types of Finishing Seals:
a. Spray-On Coatings: Spray-on coatings are convenient and easy to apply, providing a thin, even layer of protection over the metal surface. These coatings typically come in aerosol cans and can be sprayed directly onto the jewelry components. Spray-on coatings dry quickly and are suitable for use on both porous and non-porous surfaces.

b. Brush-On Lacquers: Brush-on lacquers offer more control over the application process and are ideal for intricate or delicate jewelry designs. These lacquers come in liquid form and can be applied using a brush or applicator. Brush-on lacquers provide a thicker layer of protection and are suitable for use on a variety of metals and surfaces.

c. Wax-Based Finishes: Wax-based finishes, such as Renaissance Wax or beeswax, offer a natural and traditional approach to sealing metal jewelry. These finishes are applied using a soft cloth or brush and buffed to a shine. Wax-based finishes provide a protective layer that enhances the luster and depth of the metal while offering moderate protection against tarnish and corrosion.

Application Guidelines:
a. Prepare the Surface: Before applying the finishing seal, ensure that the metal surface is clean and free from any dirt, oils, or residues. Use a mild detergent or jewelry cleaner to remove any surface contaminants, and dry the jewelry thoroughly with a soft, lint-free cloth.

b. Apply the Sealant: Depending on the type of finishing seal you're using, follow the manufacturer's instructions for application. For spray-on coatings, hold the aerosol can approximately 6-8 inches away from the jewelry and apply a thin, even layer of sealant, moving the can in a back-and-forth motion. For brush-on lacquers, dip a clean brush or applicator into the liquid sealant and apply it evenly to the metal surface, working in small sections.

c. Allow to Dry: After applying the finishing seal, allow the jewelry to dry completely according to the manufacturer's instructions. Avoid handling or touching the jewelry until the sealant has cured fully to prevent smudges or fingerprints.

d. Buff (Optional): Once the sealant has dried, you may choose to buff the jewelry with a soft cloth or polishing pad to enhance the shine and luster of the metal surface. Use gentle, circular motions to buff the jewelry until the desired level of shine is achieved.

Maintenance:

Regular maintenance is essential to prolonging the effectiveness of the finishing seal and preserving the beauty of your jewelry. Avoid exposing sealed jewelry to harsh chemicals, abrasives, or excessive moisture, as these can degrade the sealant and compromise its protective properties. When not in use, store sealed jewelry in a dry, airtight container or jewelry box to prevent tarnish and oxidation.

Conclusion:

Finishing seals play a crucial role in protecting and preserving the beauty of your metal jewelry, ensuring that your creations remain vibrant and lustrous for years to come. By choosing the right type of finishing seal and following proper application guidelines, you can safeguard your jewelry against the effects of tarnish, oxidation, and wear, allowing you to enjoy your creations for generations to come.

Chapter: Tips for Properly Finishing and Presenting Jewelry Pieces

Properly finishing and presenting jewelry pieces is essential to showcase their beauty and craftsmanship effectively. Whether you're creating jewelry for personal enjoyment, gifting, or selling, attention to detail in finishing and presentation can elevate your pieces and leave a lasting impression on admirers. In this chapter, we'll explore valuable tips for achieving professional results in finishing and presenting your jewelry creations.

Quality Finishing Techniques:
a. Thorough Polishing: Ensure that your jewelry pieces are thoroughly polished to achieve a smooth and lustrous finish. Use polishing cloths, buffing wheels, or rotary tools with polishing attachments to remove scratches, imperfections, and oxidation from the metal surface.

b. Consistent Patination/Oxidation: If you're applying patina or oxidation to your jewelry pieces, strive for consistency in the application process. Ensure that the patina is evenly applied and that the desired color and effect are achieved across the entire piece.

c. Careful Sealing: When applying finishing sealants, such as spray-on coatings or brush-on lacquers, take care to apply them evenly and allow them to dry completely. Ensure that the sealant provides adequate protection without altering the appearance or texture of the jewelry piece.

Attention to Detail:
a. Check for Imperfections: Before presenting your jewelry pieces, carefully inspect them for any imperfections or flaws. Check for scratches, irregularities, or areas where the finishing may be uneven, and address any issues promptly.

b. Cleanliness: Ensure that your jewelry pieces are clean and free from any dust, fingerprints, or residues. Use a soft cloth or cleaning solution to remove any dirt or oils from the metal surface and handle the pieces with care to avoid leaving smudges or marks.

c. Secure Components: Make sure that all components of your jewelry pieces, such as clasps, jump rings, and earring hooks, are securely attached and functioning correctly. Test the strength and durability of the components to ensure that they can withstand normal wear and tear.

Thoughtful Presentation:
a. Packaging: Choose packaging that complements the style and aesthetic of your jewelry pieces. Consider using jewelry boxes, pouches, or display cards that reflect the quality and craftsmanship of your creations.

b. Branding: Incorporate branding elements such as logos, labels, or tags into your packaging to enhance brand recognition and create a cohesive brand identity. Personalize the packaging with handwritten notes or thank-you cards to add a personal touch to the presentation.

c. Display: When presenting your jewelry pieces for sale or exhibition, pay attention to the display presentation. Use props, stands, or display cases to showcase the pieces effectively, and arrange them in a visually appealing manner to attract attention and engage potential customers.

Conclusion:

Properly finishing and presenting jewelry pieces requires attention to detail, craftsmanship, and creativity. By mastering quality finishing techniques, paying attention to detail, and presenting your pieces thoughtfully, you can create a memorable and professional presentation that highlights the beauty and value of your jewelry creations. With careful consideration and effort, you can leave a lasting impression on your audience and inspire admiration for your work.

Chapter: Guidance on Pricing and Selling Handmade Jewelry

Selling handmade jewelry can be a rewarding venture, but determining the right pricing strategy and effectively marketing your pieces are crucial aspects of running a successful jewelry business. In this chapter, we'll provide guidance on pricing and selling handmade jewelry to help you navigate the complexities of the market and maximize the value of your creations.

Understanding Costs:
a. Material Costs: Calculate the cost of materials used to create each jewelry piece, including metals, gemstones, beads, findings, and any other components. Keep detailed records of your material expenses to accurately determine the cost of goods sold (COGS).

b. Labor Costs: Factor in the time and labor required to design, create, assemble, and finish each jewelry piece. Determine an hourly rate for your labor based on your skill level, experience, and market rates, and include this in your pricing calculations.

c. Overhead Expenses: Consider overhead expenses such as studio rent, utilities, equipment maintenance, packaging materials, marketing, and other business-related costs. Allocate a portion of these expenses to each jewelry piece to ensure that all costs are covered.

Pricing Strategies:
a. Cost-Based Pricing: Calculate the total cost of materials, labor, and overhead expenses for each jewelry piece and add a markup to determine the selling price. This approach ensures that you cover all expenses and generate a profit on each sale.

b. Market-Based Pricing: Research the market to determine the prices of similar handmade jewelry pieces sold by competitors or in similar retail channels. Use this information to set your prices competitively while considering the uniqueness and quality of your pieces.

c. Value-Based Pricing: Consider the perceived value of your jewelry pieces based on factors such as craftsmanship, design, materials, and brand reputation. Set prices based on the value that customers are willing to pay for your unique creations.

Marketing and Selling:
a. Online Platforms: Utilize online platforms such as your own website, Etsy, Amazon Handmade, or social media platforms to showcase and sell your jewelry pieces. Optimize product listings with high-quality images, detailed descriptions, and relevant keywords to attract potential customers.

b. Craft Fairs and Markets: Participate in craft fairs, artisan markets, and trade shows to reach a broader audience and engage with customers in person. Invest in eye-catching displays, signage, and promotional materials to attract attention and make a memorable impression.

c. Wholesale and Consignment: Explore opportunities to sell your jewelry pieces wholesale to retailers or through consignment agreements with boutique shops, galleries, or online marketplaces. Negotiate fair terms and pricing to ensure that both parties benefit from the partnership.

Customer Service and Satisfaction:

a. Provide excellent customer service by promptly responding to inquiries, addressing customer concerns, and processing orders efficiently. Build rapport with customers by engaging with them on social media, offering personalized recommendations, and expressing gratitude for their support.

b. Offer flexible return and exchange policies to reassure customers and encourage repeat purchases. Ensure that your jewelry pieces are well-packaged and shipped securely to prevent damage during transit and enhance the overall customer experience.

c. Seek feedback from customers to gather insights into their preferences, needs, and satisfaction with your jewelry pieces. Use this feedback to refine your designs, pricing, and marketing strategies to better meet customer expectations and drive sales.

Conclusion:

Pricing and selling handmade jewelry require careful consideration of costs, market dynamics, and customer preferences. By understanding your costs, implementing effective pricing strategies, and leveraging various marketing channels, you can maximize the value of your jewelry creations and build a successful and sustainable business. Focus on delivering exceptional craftsmanship, providing excellent customer service, and continuously refining your strategies to stay competitive in the dynamic jewelry market.

Conclusion: Recap of Key Concepts Covered in the Book

In this book, we've explored the fascinating world of jewelry making, from basic techniques to advanced methods, and from selecting materials to pricing and selling your creations. Let's recap some of the key concepts covered:

Basic Techniques: We started by delving into fundamental jewelry making techniques such as stringing, knotting, wire wrapping, and bead weaving. These techniques form the foundation of jewelry making and allow artisans to create beautiful pieces with ease.

Materials and Tools: Understanding the properties of different materials, such as beads, wires, and metals, is essential for creating quality jewelry. We discussed the various types of beads, gemstones, metals, and tools used in jewelry making, providing insights into their characteristics and uses.

Advanced Techniques: We explored advanced jewelry making techniques such as enameling, etching, granulation, and Mokume Gane. These techniques offer artisans endless possibilities for creativity and self-expression, allowing them to push the boundaries of traditional craftsmanship and create unique and innovative designs.

Design and Inspiration: Finding inspiration for jewelry designs and developing a personal style are crucial aspects of jewelry making. We provided guidance on sources of inspiration, exercises to spark creativity, and tips for developing a signature style that reflects your unique vision and personality.

Finishing and Presentation: Properly finishing and presenting jewelry pieces is essential for showcasing their beauty and craftsmanship. We discussed techniques such as polishing, patina, oxidation, and finishing seals, as well as tips for presenting jewelry in a professional and appealing manner.

Pricing and Selling: Determining the right pricing strategy and effectively marketing your jewelry are critical for running a successful jewelry business. We provided guidance on calculating costs, pricing strategies, marketing and selling techniques, and customer service practices to help artisans succeed in the competitive jewelry market.

By mastering these key concepts and techniques, jewelry makers can unlock their creativity, hone their skills, and build successful and fulfilling careers in the world of jewelry making. Whether you're a beginner exploring basic techniques or an experienced artisan pushing the boundaries of advanced methods, the journey of jewelry making is one of endless discovery, inspiration, and joy. So, embrace your passion, unleash your creativity, and let your imagination soar as you continue to explore the captivating art of jewelry making.

Chapter: Embrace Your Journey

Dear Reader,

As you reach the end of this book, I want to extend my heartfelt encouragement to you as you continue your journey into the world of jewelry making. Whether you're a beginner just starting out or an experienced artisan seeking to refine your skills, remember that every step you take is a step closer to realizing your creative vision and achieving your goals.

Jewelry making is more than just a craft—it's a journey of self-discovery, exploration, and growth. Along the way, you'll encounter challenges, setbacks, and moments of frustration, but also moments of inspiration, triumph, and joy. Embrace each experience as an opportunity to learn, adapt, and evolve as an artist.

Remember that creativity knows no bounds. Don't be afraid to experiment with new techniques, materials, and designs. Allow yourself the freedom to explore and express your unique style and voice through your creations. Trust your instincts, follow your intuition, and let your passion for jewelry making guide you forward.

Surround yourself with a community of fellow artisans, mentors, and enthusiasts who share your love for jewelry making. Seek inspiration from nature, art, culture, and the world around you. Stay curious, open-minded, and eager to learn from others, and never underestimate the power of collaboration and camaraderie in fueling your creative journey.

Above all, believe in yourself and your ability to succeed. Stay patient, persistent, and resilient in the face of challenges, and celebrate your progress and accomplishments along the way. Your journey as a jewelry maker is as unique and precious as the pieces you create, so savor every moment and embrace the beauty of the creative process.

As you continue to hone your skills, refine your craft, and share your artistry with the world, remember that the most rewarding part of the journey is not the destination, but the path you take to get there. So, keep dreaming, keep creating, and keep shining your light as you embark on this extraordinary adventure of self-expression and creativity.

Chapter: Suzanne J. Katts Speaks

As you close the final pages of this book, I want to share with you some parting words of inspiration and encouragement. My journey in the world of jewelry making has been filled with wonder, discovery, and endless possibilities, and it's my greatest hope that this book has ignited a similar sense of passion and excitement within you.

Remember that creativity is not bound by rules or limitations. It's a boundless force that flows from within, waiting to be unleashed and expressed in myriad ways. Whether you're crafting delicate beaded bracelets, intricate wire-wrapped pendants, or bold metalwork designs, know that your unique voice and vision are what make your creations truly special.

In the pursuit of your artistic endeavors, don't be afraid to take risks, make mistakes, and push the boundaries of your craft. Embrace the unknown, the unexpected, and the unconventional, for it is often in those moments of uncertainty that the most extraordinary discoveries are made.

Stay curious, stay passionate, and stay true to yourself and your artistic vision. Trust in your instincts, your intuition, and your ability to overcome any obstacle that stands in your way. And above all, never lose sight of the joy and fulfillment that comes from creating something beautiful with your own hands.

As you continue your journey as a jewelry maker, remember that the most important thing is not the destination, but the journey itself—the experiences, the lessons learned, and the connections made along the way. Cherish each moment, celebrate each accomplishment, and embrace the endless possibilities that lie ahead.

Thank you for allowing me to be a part of your creative journey. May your passion for jewelry making continue to inspire and uplift you, and may your artistic endeavors bring joy and beauty to the world around you.

With warmest regards,

Suzanne J. Katts

Glossary of Jewelry Making Terms

1. Bezel Setting: A setting technique where a metal rim or collar is formed around the perimeter of a gemstone to secure it in place.

2. Cabochon: A gemstone that has been shaped and polished into a smooth, rounded, and domed form without facets.

3. Carat: A unit of weight used to measure gemstones, with one carat equivalent to 0.2 grams.

4. Cloisonné: A decorative technique where thin wires are soldered onto a metal surface to create compartments, which are then filled with enamel.

5. Crimp Bead: A small metal bead used to secure the ends of beading wire by compressing it with crimping pliers.

6. Filigree: Intricate metalwork composed of delicate wire patterns and motifs, often used as decorative elements in jewelry.

7. Hallmark: A mark or stamp indicating the purity, quality, and authenticity of precious metals such as gold, silver, and platinum.

8. Inlay: A technique where gemstones, metals, or other materials are set into recessed areas of a metal surface to create a decorative pattern or design.

9. Karat: A unit of purity used to measure the fineness of gold, with 24 karats representing pure gold.

10. Loupe: A small magnifying lens used by jewelers and gemologists to inspect gemstones and jewelry for clarity, color, and imperfections.

11. Pave Setting: A setting technique where small gemstones are closely set together and held in place by tiny beads or prongs, creating the appearance of a paved surface.

12. Soldering: A technique used to join metal components together by melting a filler metal, known as solder, to form a permanent bond.

13. Tarnish: A darkening or discoloration that forms on the surface of metals such as silver, copper, and brass due to exposure to air, moisture, or chemicals.

14. Vermeil: A type of gold-plated sterling silver where a thick layer of gold is bonded to the silver base, resulting in a durable and lustrous finish.

15. Wire Gauge: A measurement system used to specify the diameter or thickness of wire, with higher gauge numbers indicating thinner wire.

This glossary provides a basic overview of some common terms used in the art of jewelry making, helping enthusiasts and artisans alike navigate the intricate world of jewelry craftsmanship with confidence and clarity.

JEWELRY MAMES

Bracelets
Brooches
Anklets
Cufflinks
Chokers
Pendants
Charms
Earrings
Belly Chains
Toe Rings
Hairpins
Bangles
Necklaces
Rings
Hair Accessories
Body Chains
Pins
Watches
Tie Clips
Lockets

TEMPLATES

Design Sketch Template: A blank template for sketching out jewelry designs, including space for annotations, dimensions, and notes.

Materials Checklist Worksheet: A worksheet to list and track the materials needed for each jewelry design, including metals, gemstones, beads, findings, and tools.

Color Palette Worksheet: A worksheet to explore and choose color schemes for jewelry designs, including options for gemstone colors, metal finishes, and bead combinations.

Inspiration Board Template: A template for creating an inspiration board to collect images, colors, textures, and motifs that inspire your jewelry designs.

Design Planning Worksheet: A worksheet to outline and plan each jewelry design, including concept sketches, materials list, construction steps, and finishing techniques.

Budget Tracker Worksheet: A worksheet to track expenses and budget for materials, tools, and other costs associated with jewelry making.

Timeline Planner: A planner to schedule and organize tasks and deadlines for each jewelry design project, including research, design, production, and marketing.

Inventory Management Template: A template to track inventory of materials, tools, finished pieces, and work in progress, including quantities, costs, and storage locations.

Customer Feedback Form: A form to gather feedback and comments from customers about your jewelry designs, quality, pricing, and customer service.

Marketing Plan Template: A template to create a marketing plan for promoting and selling your jewelry designs, including target audience, marketing channels, promotions, and sales goals.

These templates and worksheets can help you plan, design, create, and market your jewelry pieces more effectively, allowing you to organize your ideas, manage your resources, and track your progress as you develop your jewelry making skills and grow your business.

FUTURE BOOK TITLES

Title: "Advanced Jewelry Techniques: Mastering the Art"
Description: Building upon the foundational knowledge shared in "Jewelry Making Book," this advanced guide delves deeper into complex techniques such as enameling, stone setting, and advanced metalworking. Expand your repertoire and elevate your craftsmanship to new heights with step-by-step instructions and inspiring projects.

Title: "The Artisan's Handbook: Design Principles for Jewelry Making"
Description: Unlock the secrets of design excellence with this comprehensive handbook. Learn how to create balanced compositions, harmonize colors and textures, and develop your unique artistic voice. Packed with practical advice and creative exercises, this book is your indispensable companion for cultivating your design skills.

Title: "Jewelry Business Essentials: From Passion to Profit"
Description: Turn your passion for jewelry making into a successful business venture with this essential guide. From branding and marketing to pricing and selling strategies, author Suzanne J. Katts provides invaluable insights and expert advice to help you navigate the business side of the jewelry industry and achieve entrepreneurial success.

Title: "Mixed Media Magic: Exploring New Horizons in Jewelry Making"

Description: Break free from traditional techniques and unleash your creativity with mixed media jewelry making. From incorporating textiles and found objects to experimenting with resin and polymer clay, this book inspires you to push boundaries and create truly unique wearable art pieces that dazzle and delight.

Title: "Global Inspirations: Cultural Influences in Jewelry Design"
Description: Embark on a journey around the world as Suzanne J. Katts explores the rich tapestry of cultural influences in jewelry design. Discover the symbolism, traditions, and techniques of various cultures, and learn how to incorporate them into your own designs to create meaningful and culturally resonant pieces.

Printed in Great Britain
by Amazon

7dce37bd-730a-4438-8149-76f85f4b6c21R01